A ROUND OF
GOLF COURSES

AROUND IN
GOLF COURSES

A ROUND OF
GOLF COURSES

A Selection of the Best Eighteen

by

PATRIC DICKINSON

With a Foreword by
BERNARD DARWIN

A & C BLACK · LONDON

First published in 1951 by
Evans Brothers Ltd

Published in paperback in 1990,
with the permission of
Unwin Hyman Ltd, by
A & C Black (Publishers) Ltd
35 Bedford Row, London WC1R 4JH

© 1951 Evans Brothers Ltd
© 1990 A & C Black (Publishers) Ltd

ISBN 0 7136 3238 0

A CIP catalogue record for this book is
available from the British Library

Printed and bound in Great Britain
by William Clowes Limited,
Beccles and London

CONTENTS

DEDICATED TO
ALL MEMBERS
PAST, PRESENT, AND FUTURE
OF
THE OXFORD AND CAMBRIDGE GOLFING SOCIETY

ILLUSTRATIONS
(between pages 96 and 97)

Aberdovey: 3rd Green from path to 4th tee: The Cader bunker and periscope on tee in background. (*M. H. Edwards*)

Carnoustie: Approaching 5th Green, 6th hole behind with practice field beyond. (*Sport & General*)

Ganton: The 11th from the tee. (*Yorkshire Post*)

Gleneagles: view of 14th fairway, King's Course. (*Railways Hotel Executive*)

Hoylake: The 13th—'The Rushes'. (*Guy B. Farrar*)

Hunstanton: 1st Green with 2nd tee in the foreground. (*E. E. Swain*)

Little Aston: The 17th Green as seen for the approach shot. (*Cater's News Agency*)

Moortown: The short 8th. (*Bertram Unne*)

Muirfield: The 4th from the tee. (*G. W. Day*)

North Berwick: 14th Green from top-left of ridge over which blind second must be played. (*G. W. Day*)

Portrush: 5th hole. Players walking on line of drive. Green to right, by fence on sea-edge. (*L'Atelier*)

St. Andrews: The Road hole, seen at right angles to the line of play. 18th Green and Club house in background. (*Cowie*)

Sunningdale: The 10th, from the tee. (*Marshall's*)

Walton Heath: The short 17th from behind the tee. (*Sport & General*)

Westward Ho! The rushes (*J. A. Insley*)

Worlington: The second shot to the 6th. (*R. P. W. Green*)

FOREWORD

M R. DICKINSON has done me the very pleasant honour of asking me to write a brief foreword to his book. When I agreed to do so it was on the assumption that no Cambridge golfer would leave Worlington out of his chosen round, and I was delighted to find him worthy of his bringing up. Here is Worlington at full length with its row of fir-trees, and its short hole to which the eleventh at St. Andrews is child's play, and all its other great qualities, on which we of Cambridge insist sometimes perhaps to excess. But Mr. Dickinson has seen them with entirely fresh eyes and his description owes nothing to any that have gone before. When I found that not merely had he ended with Worlington but begun with Aberdovey, I was convinced that all the courses in between would be well worth reading, and so they are. Though one knows them all well, yet the author has found so many new things to say of them that I feel rather like the man who admired Shakespeare: "Things come into his head that would never come into mine." His strong point seems to me, if I may respectfully say so, to be in his atmospherics; he can make us feel the particular wind that blows on each individual heath and the flavour of the lunch in each individual club house.

There must be gaps in the book, since there are far more than eighteen courses worthy to be sung; but Mr. Dickinson is entirely disarming on this point and he has, I admit, distributed his favours on a fair geographical basis. I did "murmur a little sadly" at finding no Prestwick, since the Seahedrig and the Cardinal and the Pow Burn must appeal to the romantic and poetical golfer that is in him.

But I am now content to believe that this is only a morning round and that there will come another just as good after lunch.

BERNARD DARWIN

INTRODUCTION

IN the year 1848, when revolutions were sweeping the face of Europe, a bloodless revolution was taking place in Scotland. Since the Middle Ages, Scots had played at the gowff, goff, or golf with sewn leather-covered balls stuffed with feathers. (There is a delightful description of the making of them in Thomas Mathison's poem "The Goff", 1743.) They were horribly expendible and expensive. On a wet day the leather got soggy and the seams burst: Scotland is not a dry country. You could use five in a round, and they cost, then, almost the same price as golf balls do now! Moreover, a smooth-surfaced ball does not rise in the air. Gowff was a tough and troglodytic experience.

But in 1848 gutta-percha, which my dictionary defines as " a greyish horny substance of inspissated juice of various Malayan trees", appeared in the West, and was made by the inventive Scots into golf balls. Because it was gum, the more it was hammered in the shop and bashed around the links the better it became. You will find the best makers advertised "all balls six-months matured"—like wine. The gutty was hard enough to retain markings upon its surface and these were found to cause it to rise. It was weatherproof and nearly indestructible, it was revolutionary! From being a highly skilled, slightly penitential exercise, golf became a pleasurable pastime.

The change took twenty years or so to cross the border. Westward Ho! was laid out, Hoylake followed. From then on to the turn of the century golf became a craze. It swept through England, and on the tide of Victorian Empire penetrated to the edges of the world, and even reached Wales. There were golf-jokes in *Punch*, golfing-verses in the magazines; 'golf-widows' trailing round in widow's tweeds; golf-books and golf-writers. But for the gutty, my dedication should run, this book would never have been written.

Naturally, in the period 1870–1900, most of the great golf courses were laid out, though they bear little resemblance to their grandchildren of 1950. But resemble them they do. Cut away the mutton-chop whiskers, the Dundrearies and Piccadilly Weepers of our own grandfathers, and they look pretty like us. So with the golf courses: the whins and heather and bent have been shaven away, but the terrain, the family characteristic, remains.

The invention of the rubber-cored ball was not in the same way a revolution. It was like the passing in aeronautics from internal combustion to jet-propulsion. But the Gutty meant Flight itself.

II

In choosing an arbitrary eighteen 'best' golf courses to describe I suppose some explanation must be given unless one intends to seek a martyr's death; which I do not, for I hope to spend happy hours at—say—Deal or Brancaster or Troon. But they are not in this book. But Hunstanton and Rye are. . . . Personal preference based on sentiment? Well, why not? But let's examine the problem further. If a reader were to visit each one of the courses in this book he would find himself—save at Ganton—within reasonable distance of at least one other fine golf course. I chose one course to represent each area, a course also which was among the finest of its kind: seaside, park, heather-and-birch, etc.

For example, Rye. If you get tired of Rye—if you *could* get tired of Rye—Littlestone is only a few miles along the coast. And the whole south-east corner of England glows emerald with Deal, and St. George's. For the south-west, Westward Ho! was essential. (It's a thousand pities Saunton was smashed up in the war: may it live again soon!) Not *too* far away is that grand links at Burnham.

London golfers mayn't agree with my choice of Sunningdale and Walton Heath. What about Wentworth, Moor Park, etc., etc.? Well, if I give you a couple of really good yardsticks, all the better to judge for yourself.

The Midlands is not perhaps ideal golfing country. Little Aston, to my mind, is the perfect example of a park course. And if you go there, they'll say, "But have you played on . . . ?" and tell you of others. And so on; I needn't enumerate and note on each course. Wherever you are you will be within reach of other golf courses perhaps not so good, perhaps better. Perhaps it all depends how well you are playing at the time. Readers may notice that I have more or less confined my Scottish golf to the east coast. I have done so with no intention of slighting the west. But the golfer visiting Scotland for the first time must go to St. Andrews, and he is likely to confine his holiday to one coast or the other. So, please, West of Scotland readers, bear with me.

If I may do so here, without offence, I would like to remind intending visitors that many of our oldest golf clubs (whether in my chosen eighteen or not) are still essentially *clubs*, and that it is always well worth writing a line to the secretary to find out whether any form of introduction is necessary. It is my own happy experience that golf-club secretaries are the kindest and most helpful body of men. They may brood over their courses like nesting birds and therefore do not like being suddenly surprised (of course they don't *really* like anyone to *play* on those smooth, beautiful expanses of grass and spoil them with divots and anger) but, taking the rough with the fairway, they put up with the members and visitors remarkably tolerantly.

I would like, then, to thank most sincerely the secretaries and committees of the clubs I have visited for their help and hospitality. To sum up: this book is intended to act as a kind of arm-chair caddy. (Corporeal caddies are a species now almost extinct, more's the pity.) The weakness of my descriptive powers will soon become apparent to the reader, but I hope I may give the line to one or two golfers, who will then go and see for themselves.

One final word. This book may also lead to the pleasant pastime of list-making. But *don't* send your *lists-of-other-18's* and your *why-have-you-left-out's* to me. I've done them all already!

ABERDOVEY

IF one dare write about Aberdovey at all, one must begin by letting Bernard Darwin through on the way to the first tee. For this links is 'his', and it is all and more than one would expect from a writer and golfer of such style; for it is both a 'classical' and 'romantic' links. It is classically narrow, requiring not coarse, gross, thumping length but a precise *accuracy* of placing the well-hit tee shot—there is that kind of striking a balance between length and line which one finds, so to speak, in the couplets of Alexander Pope. Perhaps this is going rather a long way round to say that Aberdovey has many two-shot holes and that all of them are good and two or three superlatively so.

But if you drive off the line,

> *When sorrows come, they come not single spies,*
> *But in battalions*

for the fairways are lined with battalions of small foot-high rushes —not, indeed, single spies—but all the way: and you will find counter-espionage work with your No. 8 exhausting and expensive. Yes; the secret of Aberdovey is the straight (placed) drive.

And then at the 3rd . . . the third hole is called 'Cader' because you hit over the curve of a mountainous dune into air, into thin air: so subterranean is the tee in relation to the green that you have a periscope to put you on to the target. A Coleridgean opium-dream of a hole such as Kubla Khan might easily have decreed; over the brow of 'Cader' is a 'romantic chasm' of appalling size through which, if once in, the doomed golfer will proceed with fast, thick pants, and from which I am sure that ancestral voices have prophesied far worse than war. Beyond this waste, which has its hell-gate perpendicularly guarded with railway sleepers, lies the green in a nice, friendly hollow. If you hit your tee shot straight, and far enough, the hole is an easy 3. If not, well, 33 has gone on to a medal card. For the bottom is not mere sand, but shale and stones as well. When you have finished 'Cader' you ring a bell, and I found myself involuntarily muttering,

> Hear it not, Duncan[1] ; for it is a knell
> That summons thee to Heaven or to Hell . . .

No doubt to the modern golf-architect this hideous Caliban of a creature, like its more gentle dam the 14th at Harlech, should be done away with. I do not agree. To the end of golf—till the whole game is played mechanically and golfers sit like telephone operators before switchboards in underground club houses radio-controlling their robots—let 'Cader' lose no stone. This shocking vision came to me after 'Cader' perhaps because, of all links, Aberdovey is the most perfect 'natural' golf. Old-fashioned, even antique—and so becoming immeasurably valuable. Dynamic shafts, supersonic balls, cannot avoid this basic fact: that golf is a game of skill, a game played with the head and the hands, and nothing but skill will do at Aberdovey.

The hills, here, come down almost to the shore and the links is upon a far narrower strip of land, nomansand, than at Harlech. It is shaped rather like a badly tied bow tie, with the knot far nearer one end than the other, or like a figure of 8 laid horizontally, and the knot, the wasp-waist, is the green of 'Cader' going out and the green of the 16th coming in.

Twelve holes, therefore, lie on the other side of the knot where the mountains turn away and the terrain behind the sandhills widens out considerably. Buzzards circle and squeal round the hill-tops with their bleating-mewing cries, and if it were not for the little railway that runs all the way along the landward side of the links, following the hill-foot, the scene would be very desolate and wild. All the centre of the links here is reeds and wild iris and oystercatchers looking for worms. The holes out, on the moun-tainy, railway side, have their spies on the right: and as the 7th doglegs to the right anyway, it is as well to keep leftish—there is most room. These three holes, if any are to be singled out for blame, are the pedestrian ones, but it is here also that one is likely

[1] No reference is intended to Lieut.-Colonel A. A. Duncan, the Welsh international.

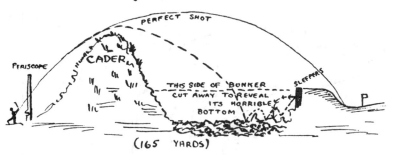

3rd hole, Aberdovey
rough Cross-section

PERFECT SHOT
PERISCOPE
CADER
THIS SIDE OF BUNKER
CUT AWAY TO REVEAL
ITS HORRIBLE
BOTTOM
SLEEPERS

(165 YARDS)

to meet as moving hazards, the little black cattle that have grazing rights and whose cloven hooves Colonel-Bogey the bunkers. Do not therefore mistake the posts along the right-hand side of the 8th for direction posts—they are rubbing-posts for the beasts (you will notice that the flag-posts are sprung for the same reason). These cattle do make keeping the links a little harder, but add to the general carefree air in which Mr. Darwin and his contemporaries played and founded the game. I find it an air incredibly restoring and reviving to breathe.

For my part I am always longing to get to the eleventh hole. From then on the links has no flaw. The 11th is one of the best two-shot holes there is, the angle from the tee being as delicate or as daring across the rushes as you like. And your pleasure in achieving it is sheer aesthetic delight—this is not a drive you simply make, it is a drive you create. Here is Aberdovey's real secret—it is truly *creative* golf. Sound craftsmanship will get you round, but creativeness will make the good round an exaltation, the bad round a despair. I can think of nowhere else that gives quite this kind of feeling; and I like to think it may have shaped Mr. Darwin's prose style too—direct, erudite, witty, and generous. For Aberdovey's greens are for the most part flat or concave and placed in a gentle bower of small hummocks, so that the just-off-the-line shot is shouldered directly inwards, the worse-off outwards. Once on the green you should never, never take three putts; they are not large undulant queries but small and simple full-stops.

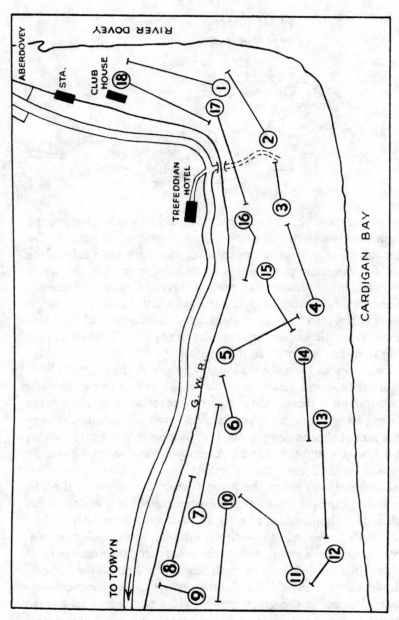

ABERDOVEY—Plan of course

I find all the second nine, enchanting holes to play. They come in along the seaward side, rushes for the hook and dunes for the slice at the long, long 13th; the same again for the 14th, slant inwards to the 15th, and then another glorious and unique hole, the 16th.

The tee is set alongside the railway line, which curves out and away again in a gentle long arc: the fairway runs likewise in a 'banked' curve, as on a motor-race track, but as the curve continues, pits, shelves, and a crater appear for the too cautious railway avoider. The straight line is just over the track in exactly the same proportions as the string of a bow if you produce it a little beyond the top end of the wood. The green is cut into the hill-side and falls away very sharply to the left. A very long dead-straight drive could reach the green. A pressed just-too-hooked drive will end very near the railway fence (or over it); a sliced drive will crash over the rim of the banking into trouble.

The thing to do is to take a cleek[1] or a baffie[2] and place it a little right of straight and short; pitch-and-run the second over the right-hand entrance to the green, and a gentle declivity will draw you in to the hole—and a putt for a 3. It is not in the nature of many temperaments to do so, and more 5's and 6's are scored at this bewitching hole than at any other.

The 17th and 18th along the railway side are flat, almost lush in comparison and it is interesting to see how these two holes, the 3rd and 16th, in the narrows, like Scylla and Charybdis, may wreck the outward-bound, hopeful, voyager; or, worse still, that rich argosy of 4's and 3's almost in sight of home.

A ditch all across the 18th will inexorably sink the straggling survivor whose head is already in a club-house cloud.

A round at Aberdovey is always a brave and gay adventure, whatever the wind's quarter.

[1] No. 1 iron.   [2] No. 4 wood.

ABERDOVEY

SCORE CARD

Hole	Yards	S.S.S.	Hole	Yards	S.S.S.
1	429	4	10	425	4
2	330	4	11	355	4
3	165	3	12	138	3
4	374	4	13	546	5
5	195	3	14	406	4
6	334	4	15	460	5
7	474	5	16	272	4
8	338	4	17	425	4
9	165	3	18	445	5
Out	2804	34	In	3472	38
			Out	2804	34
			Total	6276	72

LOCAL RULES

(Subject to St. Andrews Rules, 1934.)

1. Out of bounds, penalty distance only, means
(a) All ground north of the railway fence.
(b) All ground outside the fence at the 9th hole.
(c) The Club Houses including their verandas and gardens.

2. All ditches on the links may be treated as water hazards whether wet or dry.

3. Rushes and iris (not marram grass) are hazards.

4. A ball lying in a rabbit scrape on any part of the course, except in bunkers or hazards, may be lifted and dropped behind the scrape within a club's length without penalty. A ball lying in a rabbit burrow in a hazard may be dropped in the hazard behind the burrow without penalty.

5. When a player's ball lies on a putting green other than that to which he is playing, he must lift and drop it to one side, but not nearer to the hole.

6. A ball played into a ditch running lengthwise along the course from the tee to the green may be dropped either side within two clubs' length, and not nearer the hole, penalty 1 stroke.

7. Manure is added to the obstructions mentioned in Rule 11, R. & A., i.e. the ball may be lifted and dropped, without penalty, as near as possible to the place where it lay, and must come to rest not nearer to the hole.

8. The cart track at the 15th and 16th holes is a hazard.

CARNOUSTIE

O! It is excellent
To have the giant's strength, but it is tyrannous
To use it like a giant.
                              ("Measure for Measure.")

NOBODY could claim that the little town of Carnoustie has beauty or presence. It is a small watering-place set in a sandy bay which is absolutely safe bathing for children; indeed it is a perfect resort for toddlers, paddlers, and sandcastlers. It is an unpretentious, friendly spot, ideal for a family holiday. You expect it to have a nice little golf course that will flatter father's handicap—and you find that it has a course of real magnitude and grandeur. Big words are needed to describe this course. It is on the big scale. No professional has broken 70 there in two championships. Henry Cotton won his second championship there in 1937 with probably the greatest golf the Maestro has ever played.

Do not let this introduction frighten you away. Carnoustie is *not* fiendishly difficult: oddly enough it becomes more difficult the better player you are, which is an excellent state of affairs. It is certainly long, but it is in no sense a grind, and it is pleasant to win your match by 3 up and 2, as we shall see, not only because the 16th is near home.

There is a tremendous sense of spaciousness, without gross width. I mean that the course covers a vast tract of sandy country and that it moves round to every point of the compass in a long loping and striding way. It is not at all an out-and-homer. You do not more than nod two or three times to the players ahead of you. Yes, it is a giant of a course, and like a giant it can flick you to perdition with its little finger. But on the whole it is a friendly giant who prefers not to show his strength but to defeat you by wiles which one would, rather, attribute to a midget—by cunning changes of direction, by narrowing, subtle ditches, and by the winding of the Barry Burn. Its bunkers are all placed for the longer hitter, beautifully placed too, but there are not too many of them. The first quirk—which only a giant could get away with—is a little round pot bunker slap in the middle of the second fairway!

But we must begin at the beginning, at the bottom of the bean-stalk. About fifty yards in front of the first tee is the Burn. You can top into it easily. It is not in the least forbidding, only you *know it is there*, and you have already recognised that you will have to pitch over it to reach the 18th. There's plenty of room, and your second, or maybe third, goes blind over the end of a gently rising fairway into an old-fashioned, helpful bowl green. (The Carnoustie greens are not too formidable; they are medium-sized to small, and beautifully true—it is the play *to* the greens which will undo you—once on, you should soon be in.)

The first hole is fairly kind. So is the second—save for this fiendish central bunker, like the Cyclops' eye, glaring at you and diddling you into a wild slice or pull, when all you need is a *straight* drive, but placed to the left of it—not the right—for preference. The fairway runs along a beautiful gully among the dunes. It is here you realise why Carnoustie has a professional and an amateur par.[1] And it is here the first hint is given of its real character—for you can get home in two shots for a 4 but the second will be a long, long iron; and as the round proceeds you will find many of these longer iron shots are needed to get your 4's.

The third hole is called 'Jockie's Burn' and Jockie's Burn defends the green from any frontal attack by ground forces. This hole is a drive and an obligatory pitch. The hole curves slightly right and the ground all along slopes down sideways from the sandhills, from right to left—the hole itself runs back parallel to the 2nd, but you do not see it, being well this side of the dividing sand-dune ridge.

The 4th and 5th make with this 3rd roughly an equilateral triangle. The fifth green is just by the third tee, and in the middle of this triangle is a young fir-plantation which whispers gratuitous advice. These fir-plantations, first of all, look rather strange, out of place, and artificial, but one soon accepts them, and without them

[1] Written June, 1950.

the great open space would be bleak and too forbidding. It is also possible to get into them.

The fourth hole is flat and, as one moves inland, the character of the course changes to a more heathy-heathery mixture—and save for its length, this fourth hole is a little dull. I say "for its length" because, into the prevailing west winds, it is again a long two-shotter and the green is very shy: it peeps round its bunkers like an old lady round a lace curtain. But the 5th is a beauty. It is slightly doglegged to the right, so of course there are bunkers shepherding you leftwards towards the plantation, and clean across the fairway, just where a long, straight drive reaches it—is Jockie's Burn again! So you have to drive circumspectly and adroitly—leaving yourself a longer second than you'd like to a green beautifully placed beyond the partial eclipse, on the right, of a mound with bunkers on it; and of course there are bunkers for the pulled-hopeful, avoid-trouble sort of attitude (put there for the English rather than the Scottish temperament?).

Have you so far got five professional 4's? How far up the bean-stalk are you? . . . or up the spout? . . .

The 6th is a hole to dream about. It is an epic in itself. It is 521 yards long. Along its whole length to the left, and close to the left, is an out-of-bounds fence, you can top into Jockie's Burn; there are bunkers, just reachable, in the middle of the fairway; and crowning brutality!—you will see away up the fairway, a full brassie ahead, a white post. You think, credulous that you are, that it is there merely for your help. It is in the middle of the fair-

6th hole, Carnoustie

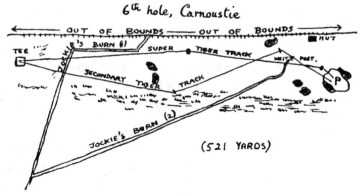

(521 YARDS)

way. Yes, it is there to help you, for it marks the end of a fiendish ditch which has insinuated itself over from the 5th, across the rough, to end here its vile career, like a poisoned rat that has died just exactly under the larder it has been wont to raid. So your second has to be directed towards a narrow gap, with the out-of-bounds leering at you more horribly than ever. You can play deliberately right, to cut shorter over the ditch, but that leaves you in heavy rough and with about an eighty-yard pitch over a nice wide bunker. Really, this is a gigantically good hole. I may have made it sound impossible, but in reality it is not at all impossible—only very, very strict to the long hitter. The longer handicap player will probably reach the green comfortably in four shrewd heaves and bolt a putt for a 5!

The 7th, another excellent two-shot hole with another fir-plantation on the right for a quick slice, and the out-of-bounds still along the left flank, takes you to the western corner of the course, the farthest from home. There used to be a fine and well-grown plantation at the back of the seventh green and running along the left of the 8th and 9th, which turn at right angles north towards the railway. But, alas, the trees were all cut down during the war and the power to replant them lies not in the hands of the golf club: the land belongs to the War Office. And so . . . There is no protection now at the short 8th—the first short hole in the round—nor at the 9th, another first-rate two-shotter, and as usual the testing length (417 yards). So much for the first nine, which the professionals are expected to shoot in seven 4's one 5, and one 3.

This corner of the course, near the railway and with the iron works' cranes and chimney just beyond, seems anything but sea-side! You *might* be in Leeds. Thank heaven, fasting, that you are not. The first hole coming in is called 'South America'. It's a strange, lush, inland kind of hole, a flat fairway and a pitch to an island green nestling in the crooked embraces of the Barry Burn. With assorted trees around it, it looks like somebody's garden. You can be in the water if you pitch short or if you cut, but the Burn is only really trying out its mesmeric powers here, which it will use later, and there is no real excuse for aquatics. This hole is called 'South America' because once upon a time—before the railway ran to Dundee—in the mid-nineteenth century, one David Nicoll decided to sell up and seek his fortune in that land. Before he set out he had a party, obviously a very good one, and starting off to walk to Dundee he got only about a mile from the town when he was, for some reason, overcome and lay down to sleep. Waking the next morning he may have believed that he had arrived, but anyway he liked where he was so much that he built himself a cottage there, with a small holding, and lived happily ever after.

Incidentally, the men of Carnoustie have always been, it seems, adventurous. For Carnoustie has an almost exclusive 'goodwill' in North America, and has carried golf to most of the round earth's four corners. It is a great nursery of golf, and since the 'nineties has scattered about three hundred teaching professionals, the true seeds of golf, to grow and bear fruit wherever the game is played. To Americans, Carnoustie is holy, for it was in copying the swing of Stewart Maiden, at Eastlake, that Bobby Jones learned to play.

I picked up my game watching him play, unconsciously as a monkey, and as imitatively. I grew up swinging so precisely like Stewart that an old friend of Stewart's mistook me for him . . .[1]

Families emigrated. Five Smiths were simultaneously professionals in the States, and it almost broke the town's heart when Macdonald Smith failed to win the Open in 1931, wrecking himself in the fatal last three holes.

America, Australia, South Africa have profited by Carnoustie's missionary zeal (as indeed have the missionaries!).

But I have left you perhaps fishing for your ball at 'South America'. Got it? Well, a little boy got it. And you gave him a penny? Good, now let's go on. All this part of the course, 7th, 8th, 9th, 11th, 12th, 13th, is of a heathy quality rather than close seaside. The turf is spongier and the rough is heather and scattered broom bushes. On a hot summer's day there's honey to smell, not salt.

We should start home, then, with a 4 at 'South America',

---

[1] From *Down the Fairway*, by R. T. Jones.

another at the 11th, and perhaps at the 12th, which is called 'Southward Ho!'.

It is from now on that the finish begins. The 13th is a very short hole (135 yards) played to a tiny tilting green with a bunker in it that makes it look like a green biscuit with one giant bite out of it. It is criminally easy to take four, and with what is to come *you must get your* 3.

From now on, we move seawards and the lies gradually 'tighten'. The 14th is a fine hole. After your drive the fairway ends with a fairly quickly rising hillock in whose face are set two bunkers: 'The Spectacles', and, paradoxically, one has to play a *blind* shot over to the green about fifty yards beyond. It often takes "three good shots to get up in two." The 15th is a really beautiful hole (I must admit that it is my favourite); all that a two-shot hole should be. The fairway is diagonally hog-backed from right to left about two hundred yards from the tee and you must play to the right, or your ball will be carried steeply down left and leave a completely blind second. Suppose you've placed your drive along the right: the ground rises, undulates, narrows to a bottle-neck, and the green is in a hollow just beyond. You need to play a longish iron shot, a wee bit left and with a shade of cut for perfection: dead straight will do. My powers of description, I know, fail lamentably to convey the shape and feel of a hole; this one has a particularly satisfying rhythm about it. The contours are so finely moulded; it is a hole with a beautiful figure; and it moves like a show-girl with poise and grace. One should dress it in the most stylish fashion one can.

Now for these last three holes, the dreaded Carnoustie finish: par is 3, 4, 5 for the professional; 3, 5, 5 for the amateur. Three successive players in the 1931 Open required par to win; each failed. In the third round Macdonald Smith took 3, 3, 4, and the Barry Burn must have wriggled almost another loop of resentment. In the last round MacSmith needed 3, 4, 5 to win. He took 5, 6, 5 . . .

The 16th is a long one-shotter (235 yards) to a small, high plateau green, straitly guarded. The tee is on another eminence, above green-level, and gives you a nice sense of freedom and room, which is illusory. Only the best shots stay there. . . .

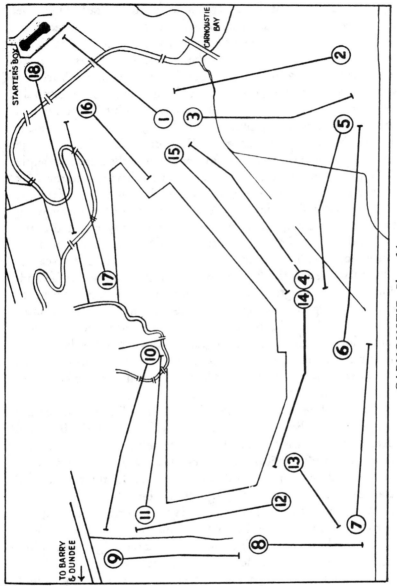

CARNOUSTIE—Plan of the course

27

The Barry Burn, at the last two holes, performs rather like one of the snakes that tangled and looped round Laocoon; it seems to be everywhere. You cross its coils and swings three times at the 17th, and twice at the 18th; and the second time it bars the entire entrance to the green: a quick hook from the eighteenth tee can get in it; a longer hook can be out of bounds; I think a slice could be caught in the loop in front of the seventeenth tee, upon which we are still standing wanting to finish 4, 5. And this tee-shot is against the prevailing west wind. Your drive should land on the 'island', over the first two wriggles and before the third: the angle of Burn and rough here is acute and you are driving into the apex of it: the farther, the narrower. It's nice, thick lush sort of rough: the sort that will strangle your club a bit, and flop your recovery shot, yes, just nicely in. . . . At least, if the wind were ahead at the 17th, now it'll be behind you, and to hell with the carry over the Burn, you're well down the fairway, you can get on in two easily. Of course there *is* the Burn to be carried, but the wind's behind, and of course the green isn't *far* beyond it, and you don't want to end up through the railings at the back, so a nice calculation must ensue. Play short, six to one you'll just over-hit it: go for it and half a dozen to the other you'll spare it . . . as usual it's that special awkward Carnoustie length of second. Gene Sarazen said he'd like to know he had a 5 to win and he would then play the hole with three iron shots!

This *dénouement* is like the climax of an Elizabethan drama: daggers are out by the 16th, a poison-cup filled from the Burn and drunk deeply at the 17th; and the eighteenth green is littered with dead bodies which Fortinbras (fresh from a 72 at St. Andrews) arrives to clear up and cart off, on trolleys . . . But it is really grand tragedy finish: or is it *grand guignol*? or a bit of both?

Whichever it is, you've got to play it in a medal round; in a match, did I not say earlier, win if you can by at least 3 and 2, unless you have nerves of steel and can do a bit of 'gamesmanship' on your opponent, on the seventeenth tee.

I do want to stress, after what seems a pretty gruelling round, that Carnoustie is a really fascinating and attractive giant "wot don't know 'is own strengf", not a malignant monster.

And if you do find it too much for you there is the shorter

'Burnside' course laid out in the giant's midriff; a very pleasant, heathery second best; shorter, easier, but in its own way extremely attractive, despite a rather gloomy stretch beside the railway.

What finally one feels about Carnoustie is that it is a course one will continually want to return to. One could not ever get tired of it, and I mean that as a great compliment. It is fierce as a lion and sweet as honey.

CARNOUSTIE

Hole	Name	Length	S.S.S.	Hole	Name	Length	S.S.S.
1	Cup	401	4	10	South America	406	4
2	Gulley	418	5	11	Dyke	352	4
3	Jockie's Burn	321	4	12	Southward Ho	467	5
4	Hillocks	365	4	13	Whins	135	3
5	Brae	363	4	14	Spectacles	473	5
6	Long	521	5	15	Luckyslap	424	4
7	Plantation	376	4	16	Barry Burn	235	3
8	Short	146	3	17	Island	428	5
9	Railway	417	5	18	Home	453	5
	Out	3328	38		In	3373	38
					Out	3328	38
					Total	6701	76

LOCAL RULES
(Revised, Carnoustie, April 1st, 1950.)

1. *Marking Posts.*—Black-and-white posts indicate 'out of bounds'. Red-and-white posts indicate 'lateral water hazards'.

2. *Out of Bounds:*

Generally.—Balls over any fence bounding the course.

Tree Plantations.—Balls in or over the furrow bounding the plantation bordering the 3rd, 4th, and 5th holes, and the plantation lying between the 7th and 14th holes.

1st Hole.—Balls in burn to left of two black-and-white indicating pins on banks of burn.

4th Hole.—In or over ditch along north side of plantation on left of fairway.

14th Hole.—Balls in or over furrow, indicated by black-and-white pins running between this hole and the 8th hole of Burnside course.

3. *Water Hazards.*—The Barry Burn, Jockie's Burn, and all ditches are water hazards. Balls may be lifted and dropped within two clubs' length of fairway edge of banks guarding such hazard, but not nearer the hole—penalty one stroke.

Lateral Water Hazards.—Section of ditch between 4th and 5th holes beyond north-west corner of plantation. (Applicable to 4th hole only.) Ditches on left of 6th, 7th, and 9th holes, near to and running parallel with Government boundary fences; ditch between 9th and 12th holes; ditch between 12th hole and Burnside course.

4. *Well Coverings, etc.*—Balls lying on well coverings, on water connections (hydrants) throughout the course, in cavity at grating at approach to 18th green, may be lifted and dropped without penalty, not more than two clubs' length from such obstruction, but not nearer the hole.

5. *Ball on another Green.*—A ball played on to a putting green, other than that of the hole being played, shall be lifted and dropped on fairway, but not nearer the hole. Should such green be adjacent, the ball may be played therefrom provided that the stroke is played with a putter—in both cases no penalty. (Definition: Putting green is any prepared putting surface.)

6. *Rabbit Holes.*—Balls lying in rabbit holes may be lifted and dropped without penalty within a radius of two clubs' length, but not nearer the hole.

GANTON

G ANTON! That name should at once signal another: Harry Vardon—perhaps the greatest of all English golfers—whose cottage is still to be seen in the little village near by. There should be a plaque over the door.

The course has not made as many protean changes, since its founding, as the great seaside links. And yet, because it is pure golfing country it has kept abreast of the game. Here, on July 22nd, 1899, with the gateposts decorated one with roses the other with thistles, Harry Vardon trounced Willie Park in the last 36 of their great 72-hole challenge match, to win the whole by 11 and 10. 'Big Crawford' (a famous itinerant caterer whose home green was North Berwick) was disappointed with the crowd, a measly two thousand or so (of course it rained), for at North Berwick, Park's home green, he had had "a bit ginger beer stall at the turn and sold a hunnert and twelve dozen that day". And here, of course, in 1949 exactly fifty years later the Americans performed prodigies of valour in the singles to win the Ryder Cup. I cannot help thinking that the sad, contemplative eyes of Vardon —there is a wonderfully good photograph of him in the dining-room—took on an even more gently reproachful look that day. Much is now written about the 'training' for such contests—it is amusing to note Crawford's comment on Willie Park: "The man's no' been pittin' on meat. He's jist been eatin' fancy stuff. He should jist dae like me, and take a guid big basin o' brose till's brakfast and a muckle baup. . . ."

Maybe our own Ryder Cup team should have done the same, for Ganton has its mailed fist under a green velvet glove. It does not forgive mistakes.

The way to arrive at it, if you can, is by car from Driffield, so that you are coming north, climbing slowly up to Foxholes, and then suddenly, over Ganton Brow, the whole wide rich valley of the River Derwent lies before you, and there away below, a positive Eldorado of golden bunkers, is the links. You drop down the steep hill-side, over the main Scarborough–York road, with Ganton village just on the right, and down alongside the 16th with its line of fir-trees in gossiping clumps, turn through that legendary gate and arrive at a club house, designed *as* a club house, and as really comfortable and accommodating as a house agent's prospectus! There is always a first-class lunch from 12.30 to 2; there is a gentlemen's wing and a ladies' wing, and between them a common dining-room and lounge.

I have lingered over the arrival at Ganton, for there is a particular flavour to it: a welcoming and yet an aristocratic greeting: an air of traditional good manners, even, is communicated from the bunkers: "Good morning", they seem to say, "we hope to be introduced"; and like many things in perfect taste it all looks rather simple and innocently straightforward.

Ganton, like Mildenhall, lies on a substratum of rich sand, and they have qualities of turf in common; but here the turf is softer and spongier, there is more grass on the fairways, and the greens are even-paced, steady-going fellows that put your putts in the hole like investments in government stock. Ganton doesn't gamble. Play steadily, play discreetly, and play with good taste and common sense. The course is like one of those well-made, close-knit sober poems from which it is impossible to pick out a purple passage—the effect is cumulative—at the end, you suddenly realise "that was really good", and you look back to discover—and read the whole poem again. So with this course, it is not easy to pick out any brilliant or romantic passages—it has no really 'quotable' holes. If there is one, my personal choice falls upon the 4th, which has a most beautifully poised green and requires a particularly accurate second shot.

To take you round such a course hole by hole, shot by shot, is like a dull teacher picking out the syntax, the grammar, and saying, "Look, because that sentence is constructed *so* (and notice the phrasing), *therefore* it is a masterpiece." In this way school teachers destroy, in their well-meaning way, the incipient powers of aesthetic appreciation in most of their pupils.

But round the course you must go, at once. The caddie-master will find you a game if he can, and anyway will welcome you and make you feel easy in your mind. What other English course still keeps up and, I must add, is able to keep up this excellent institution of the caddie-master?

What must be admitted at once is the perfection of the green-keeping. Once upon a time the word '*course*' meant the fairway; the 'course' at Ganton is, simply, a fairerway. Nature's seasonally woven patterns of buttercup, dandelion, daisy have been ruthlessly and scientifically liquidated and the grass grows 'so rich and green' that it seems to have a pile to it like a millionaire's carpet. Only a real Puritan golfer bred on the sandy austerities of the seaside could complain, and that would be a moral plea of too much indulgence leading to vice. Yes, these fairways are cosseted and pampered: they are watered in drought, and I believe that in a hard winter the secretary might cover them with straw, reserving a last few wisps for his own hair. There are grades of rough from *piano* to *fortissimo*, and a great deal of close-growing and not unobtrusive gorse: gold-red-gold of bunker, yellow-gold of gorse bloom, and olive-green of gorse prickle, and in between all shades and preciosities of green: jade, emerald, sea-green.

It would be just possible to start at Ganton with five consecutive 3's: in the Ryder Cup match "Dutch" Harrison almost did so: dropping a stroke at the 3rd, which is a one-shotter, he started 3, 3, 4, 3, 3 and got another 3 at the long 6th—and our own Dai Rees ended his thirty-six holes with something like 11 under 4's. This is fantastic: but Ganton is an extremely capricious place and the bridge between a 5 or a 3 at a par 4 is a narrow one. Essentially it is a course which favours a really delicate and accurate chipper and putter. It is not really long, and there are no really fierce carries. The secret of Ganton lies in its subtle 'use of ground' and its brilliant, suggestive bunkering.

Bunkers are of two kinds: there are the solid crushers of golfing crime, obvious as the tread of policemen's boots; these catch and deal with such old lags as the nasty short slice, the smothering quick hook; even the head-up top: but there are other bunkers: beautiful alluring sirens, daring us to steer too near them, rallying our faint hearts to carry over them, and sneering at our feebleness if we take the middle course ("middle-*aged* course" they mock). Ganton's bunkers are peculiarly sweet-singing creatures that lie about in exquisitely nonchalant attitudes, just off the line . . . a

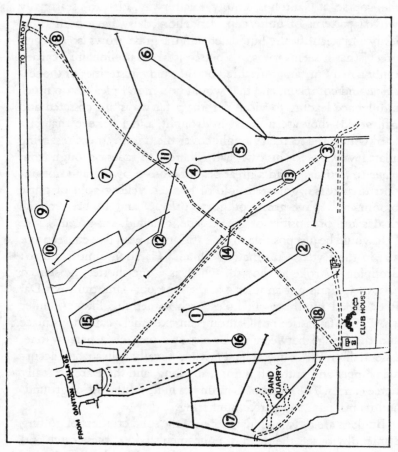

GANTON—Plan of the course

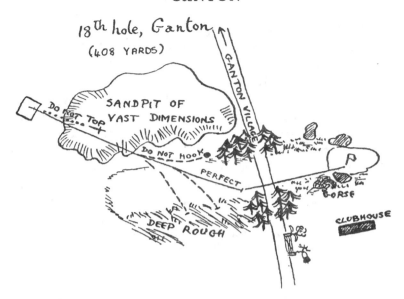

beautiful example is the long one-shot third hole; another is the 6th. But there is a great number of them and all of them welcome little golf balls in "with gently-smiling jaws".

But when Ganton goes in for a really solid crusher it does the job thoroughly: the colossal sand-pit, left of the 17th and over which you drive to the 18th, is a real life-sentence, more imposing, I think, than its compatriot at Westward Ho!

The finish at Ganton, 16th, 17th, 18th, is a great one. The 16th is a long two-shot hole alongside the road to the club. Here, again, your drive must carry a real Superintendent of a cross-bunker: there are fir-trees on the right, and a big sentinel beech-tree down on the left seems to narrow the fairway considerably. The fairway slopes gently down, and as gently up again to the green. This was the hole Americans liked most, and it is very picturesque and pretty to look at. The 17th is a very long one-shot, or drive-and-pitch, hole at right angles across the road: the immense sand-pit is well left, but will gratefully chumble up a quick hook, and a gang of sirens thumb you up the right-hand side: there's plenty of room, or there *should* be. One remembers the Mad Hatter and his two friends at that large tea-table shouting, "No room! No room !" "There's *plenty* of room !" said Alice. This is exactly the mental attitude to be in on the seventeenth tee.

The 18th is a truly awesome hole to finish. It is doglegged and you must drive as far as possible over the crater. The fairway falls away to the right sharply, and a too widely cautious stroke will be (*a*) in the rough and (*b*) out of reach of the green. But let's assume you have placed a perfect tee-shot; your second must be played between the fir-trees, the entrance to some giant's estate,[1] to a green that seems very narrow and is guarded closely along its right flank with some low gorse that seems to growl at you as if it were a dog and the green were its dinner-plate. There are bunkers. A very long drive down the left may leave you stymied by the trees: if you can finish your round with an aggregate of twelve shots for these last three holes you will be doing well enough.

I think another of Ganton's siren secrets is that as you finish you want to start again. However well you have played—you could surely do better, and out it entices you to try again, and again. For a golfing holiday—but with a car to get there—Ganton is ideal. You will never get tired of the course and it will not get tired of you.

[1] *See* Carnoustie.

GANTON

SCORE CARD

Hole	Length	S.S.S.	Hole	Length	S.S.S.
1	380	4	10	173	3
2	427	4	11	417	4
3	250	4	12	212	3
4	412	4	13	507	5
5	154	3	14	297	4
6	457	5	15	450	5
7	440	4	16	453	4
8	400	4	17	250	4
9	505	5	18	408	4
Out	3425	37	In	3167	36
			Out	3425	37
			Total	6592	73

LOCAL RULES

1. A ball is 'out of bounds' if driven over or into any of the boundary fences or ditches (i.e. fences or ditches dividing any part of the links from land not used as links. This includes the horse pasturage bounding part of the 15th hole). In or over the road is out of bounds when playing the 16th hole, but not when playing the 17th and 18th.

2. The ditches at the 4th, 5th, 12th, 13th, and the lake at the 5th and 6th (except as qualified by Local Rule 1) are defined as water hazards.

3. A ball lying on the road at the 17th and 18th holes may be lifted and dropped behind under penalty of one stroke. The road is held to include the whole area between the boundary fences on each side. If either of the wire fences interferes with a player's stroke, and the ball does not lie in the road area, the ball may be lifted and dropped not more than two clubs' length behind the wire fence farthest from the hole, without altering the line to the hole.

See Rules of Golf No. 33.

4. A ball played on to any surface prepared for putting other than that of the hole being played, or on to any practice putting green, must be lifted without penalty and dropped within two clubs' length of the edge of such putting green but not nearer to the hole being played.

5. On the day or days of a stroke competition, the course, excluding the putting greens, is defined as a practice ground with the proviso that a player practising is not permitted to play a stroke from any teeing ground or to play on to any putting green or at any hole of the stipulated round that is within his reach.

GLENEAGLES

THERE is a story of the headmaster of a very new public school, which was determined to be all that such places should be. One day he summoned all the boys together and addressed them: "Boys, I have *three new traditions* to announce. . . ." I must admit that I feel rather like that about Gleneagles. That it should be on the lips of Scots in the same breath as St. Andrews (as it is) strikes me as a little odd. Both have their place in the game, and those two places are as different as chalk used to be from cheese before cheese was nationalised.

So let us be fair from the very start; or even before the start. Gleneagles is something that was created, and exists, sheerly to please; if I may take a simile from the theatre it is glorious musical comedy. Now, I emphatically do not mean that as any sort of denigration. Good musical comedies—such as *Annie, Get Your Gun*—provide something unique and very worth while to the jaded human being. Musical comedies provide humour (sometimes unconscious), spectacle, fantasy, gaiety, and a mad champagne effervescence; life is not like this—nor would it be bearable if it were—but to pretend it is, for a little while, is heavenly. If you care to substitute the word 'Golf' for 'Life' and read that sentence again you will be half-way up the drive which leads to Gleneagles.

Here is 'streamlined' golf. The word 'streamline' itself has taken on a very different meaning from the first days when only designers and engineers used it. We know what it means now. Add the word 'chromium' and you are even nearer the first tee; and remember that, now, you *own* Gleneagles! For the course belongs to the Hotel, the Hotel to British Railways, and British Railways to you. And for this you have the choice—such as the old railways gave you—of three classes: the King's Course, the Queen's, and the Prince's, which—may I be forgiven for suggesting—would better have been called the Knave's—that is, from the golfer's point of view.

The origin of Gleneagles is a railway one. In the great pre-1914 railway days, when railways were small competitive concerns, there was a Caledonian Railway which advertised "True to time trains which, readily covering distance on measured speed, bring Delightful Districts within the range of Daily Travelling with true convenience, true comfort and true economy and conclusively establish The Caledonian Railway in the becoming title The True Line to Country Life". But, alas, country life was not enough. Other railways had their hotel-and-golf course; there was Turnberry, Cruden Bay . . . and one day a Director of the Caledonian alighted at Crieff Junction to observe unspoiled country life in the region of Strathearn, between Blackford and Auchterarder. He looked south to the Ochil Hills, he looked north to the foothills of the Grampians. He looked more closely at the heathery, tussocky moor. What was that glen, in the Ochils there, where the road goes through to Dunfermline and Edinburgh? Gleneagles? Gleneagles! This was the perfect place, and perfect name. Here should be the hotel to end all hotels and the golf course—course? *Courses* . . . I will not repeat the catchphrase! Crieff Junction was renamed Gleneagles. The ground was surveyed, the site was chosen. The most famous golfer and golf-course designer of the day should lay out the course. James Braid was summoned to improve upon and to tame Nature. . . .

The First World War slowed down but did not stop this great work, and in 1919 an obelisk or cairn was raised on a small hillock (which we shall learn to call a 'wee law' before long) and a stone was inserted in it, reading: "Gleneagles Golf Course, opened in 1919, the year of the peace after the Great War".

The motto of Gleneagles, inscribed upon a device which looks not unlike some form of ex-service badge, is *Heich abune the Heich*, the translation of which is not "Hiccup upon Hiccup" but "High above the High". Gleneagles *is* high up. The 'Tappit Hen', once a measure for spirits or claret corresponding to a quart, and now the name of the twelfth hole, stands 614 ft. above sea-level. This is not altogether an advantage, because the views are often obscured in what the Scots call mist and the English call steady soaking rain. However, when the clouds lift, the views are indeed magnificent. At Gleneagles we are not asking for great golf, but thoroughly delightful, pleasant, unexacting golf: the fairways and greens are almost too true to be good and the views almost too good to be true. Like Ophelia,

Thought and affliction, passion, hell itself,
She turns to favour and to prettiness.

Everything at Gleneagles is favourable and pretty. The prospects from the tees are delicious, the fairways are soft, mossy, and re-silient, and if ever Euclid had played golf here, he would have spent the time calculating whether they were as broad as they are long as they are broad. These courses are the golf architect's dream, and I must be forgiven if I recount here that a colonial golf architect going from Gleneagles, which he thought the per-fectest course in the world, to Muirfield, suggested that Muirfield should be planted with strategic and picturesque clumps of trees! If only Dr. Syntax, who set out so resolutely in search of the Picturesque in the eighteenth century, had had Gleneagles to visit! But in the twentieth century there is Mr. Fitzpatrick, that maker of technicolor travelogue films . . . he should visit this place and have a long, slow, lush technicolor sunset down the glen as his finale (the glen is roughly due south). But at Gleneagles everything is roughly due south. This is a place the Scot is "sel-ling" to the English, and it is too seldom that one hears a Scottish voice. Here repair, to repair themselves, magnates from the ravages that Leeds makes upon the system; tycoons from Man-chester; brokers from Golders Green; and always a ground bass of those for whom good advertisement has an irresistible appeal. I myself think that a non-stop luxury helicopter service between Gleneagles and Brighton would be likely to pay . . . under private enterprise.

What I cannot understand is why the flags are simple white and red. With every Scottish tartan crying out to be used, it seems something the founders missed.

There are, then, three courses at Gleneagles. The King's is the longest, the Queen's the prettiest, and the Prince's has only nine holes.

Here is the antithesis to the heavenly hurly-burly of St.

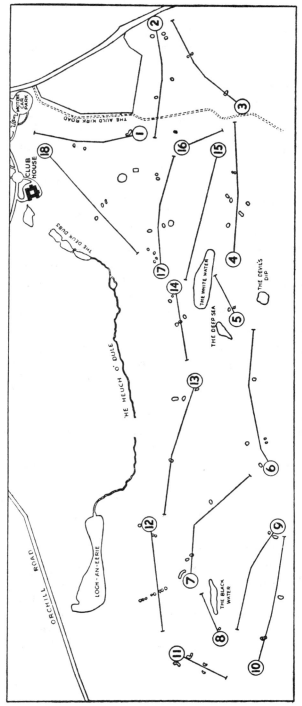

GLENEAGLES—Plan of King's Course

Andrews. All is discreet. Each hole is laid out so that, if possible, patrons shall not see other patrons, but feel that the course is theirs alone. Adroit use of valleys and defiles is responsible. As at the old Japanese Embassy, where there were cupboards on the stairs that servants could retire into when the Great Ones ascended or descended, one feels that here, at Gleneagles, the caddies should proceed through a series of mole-runs, just coming up to hand the club and disappearing again, until the eighteenth greens: King's Hame and Queen's Hame. Golf at Gleneagles takes us too near London, and not near enough Edinburgh. Those who know that classic book *England, Their England* by A. G. Macdonell, should study the chapter on golf with zeal before appearing here, remembering, too, that the Honourable Company of Edinburgh Golfers were betting in 'corners' in the eighteenth century.

'Relax' is the word. Ree-lax. There is a pathetic reference to the rough in a brochure of 1921 in which it is recorded that Braid uttered a stern admonition, "Ye shouldna' be there". Perhaps there was more rough then, but now it is, frankly, almost an impossibility to "be there".

No, it is not. I've witnessed many brave attempts at discovery.

But, please, tell us—is it good golf? Why is it that Gleneagles has a kind of awful J. M. Barrie compulsiveness and asks-to-be-visited?

Well, it is, truly, set in marvellous surroundings. The views, (see back,) are really very, very pretty, like a Scottish scene on a box of chocolates. And inside are precisely forty-five lovely chocs, two layers of 18, one of 9, and all without exception are quite delicious and you can't help going on taking them. What is an evening out at the musical theatre without the rustle of choccy papers in the quieter moments? But be serious. What is Gleneagles?

First and foremost it is a fine tract of inland golfing country most exquisitely kept in order. It is absolutely first-rate of its kind. The greens are as good inland greens as anywhere in the kingdom; thick, lush, true, ideal for the good bold putter and the pitch-up-and-stopper. Pitch-and-runs don't pay, there's too much pile on the carpet. Through the green there is, for the reasonably straight player, nothing but fairway, nothing but good springy sit-up-and-hit-me kind of lies. The bunkers are placed for the rabbit rather than the good golfer. (Talking of rabbits, I think it the perfect paradox that Bishop Hamilton should have made a charter with St. Andrews to *breed* rabbits, provided the inhabitants were let play golf. Had he negotiated with Gleneagles now, the terms might have been reversed. Breed golfers and we will farm the rabbits. . . .)

There is nothing to prevent the steady fourteen handicap player from breaking, or nearly breaking, 80 on the King's Course; or the Queen's, where there are six short holes to help. There's 3 under 4's, surely, and only twelve holes to play.

Now let us emphasise that it *is* really intensely pleasant to play at Gleneagles. The golf is never dull, it always looks attractive, and it is; and often looks happily, a little *more* difficult than it is which is heartening, and golfers as a tribe do need heartening.

Only the most curmudgeonly of creatures could ask for more.

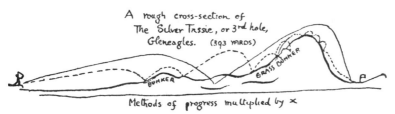

A rough cross-section of The Silver Tassie, or 3rd hole, Gleneagles. (393 YARDS)

Methods of progress multiplied by x

Do not, I repeat, go to Gleneagles expecting stern, championship golf. Go expecting to be entertained continually, flattered, delighted, feasted. You will come away as from your musical comedy with a tune or a snatch of what you did really well, of what you saw, and of how enchanting it all was.

Forget, I counsel you, the Scottish phoney which was laid on for advertisement purposes. These awful names for the holes which few Scotsmen can translate for you, and the general air of music-hall-tartan which overhangs the place.

Golf for the majority of those who play it is a bit of a trial. Shots do go astray. Here is the ideal salve. There are, I think, too many blind shots and trick shots, such as the second shot over a high, a too high, 'law' at the third hole, but it is all good fun, and it is extremely jolly and rewarding.

There's nothing like Gleneagles. Ballyhoo apart, it *has* managed to create a spirit of its own which is neither a haze of pink gins nor a "wee doch an' doris"—that is, a spirit of real carefreedom. A swat from the first tee on the King's is a freer swat than anywhere else I know.

Let me repeat, it is ravishingly pretty. Pansies grow wild on the fairways in their season, and there is a profusion of other flowers. You can hear the 'wheepling o' the whaups' any day, if you can recognise curlews, and there are grouse and black-cock too. The view to Blackford from the seventh fairway of the Queen's Course is a view that was there before the Queen's Course was, and is inviolable.

I'm sure you will enjoy playing the Kittle Kink, the Heich o' Fash, or the Witches' Bowster, and the Denty Den is a really "canny wee holie the noo". So here's to every braw gowffer and rank is but the guinea stamp an' a man's a man for a' that.

For a' that, Gleneagles is one of the wonders of the golfing world, a kind of hanging garden of Babylon on a Scottish hillside, and if you marry Golf, here's the place to spend your Hinny Mune![1]

[1] Honeymoon.

44

GLENEAGLES

Hole	Name	Length	S.S.S.	Hole	Name	Length	S.S.S.
1	Dun Whinny	370	4	10	Canty Lye	457	5
2	East Neuk	405	4	11	Deil's Creel	195	3
3	Silver Tassie	393	4	12	Tappit Hen	402	4
4	Broomy Law	478	5	13	Braid's Brawest	465	4
5	Het Girdle	171	3	14	Denty Den	285	4
6	Blink Bonnie	474	5	15	Howe o'Hope	465	4
7	Kittle Kink	455	4	16	Wee Bogie	151	3
8	Whaup's Nest	175	3	17	Warslin' Lea	390	4
9	Heich o'Fash	372	4	18	King's Hame	474	4
	Out	3293	36		In	3284	35
					Out	3293	36
					Total	6577	71

LOCAL RULES

King's Course:

A ball is out of bounds if it lies beyond the wire fence to the left of the 1st, 6th, and 10th holes, or behind the 2nd green.

A ball in the ditch dividing the 9th and 10th fairways may be lifted and dropped under penalty of one stroke.

General:

If a ball is on a putting green other than that of the hole being played, the ball must be lifted and placed, without penalty, within two clubs' length of the green, but not nearer the hole.

If a ball lies within two clubs' length of a fixed seat, shelter, guide post, notice board, or hydrant cover, and such obstacle interferes with the stroke, the ball may be lifted and dropped, without penalty, at any spot within two clubs' length thereof, but not nearer the hole.

A ball in a cart road can be lifted and dropped without penalty.

If a ball lies or be lost in water (other than casual water), the player may drop a ball, under penalty of one stroke, within two clubs' length of the spot at which the ball entered the water.

If a ball lies in a rabbit scrape, so that a club laid across the top of it does not touch the ball, the ball may be lifted and dropped without penalty. This rule also applies to bunkers.

HARLECH
Royal St. David's

———————◇———————

I CANNOT believe that there is any links in the world set in more romantically beautiful surroundings than Harlech.

From the battlements of Harlech castle on the great grey stone cliffs you look down, down, to a flat sea-sandy plain below, itself defended from the sea by colossal sand-dunes; you see the whole sweeping curve of the bay northwestwards, and looking north the indented line of Snowdonia like the serrated back of some vast ancient saurian monster, which changes colour with every mood of the elements. Looking down from the castle, you see those yellow pockmarkings and vivid slug-like green trails which mean golf. Having descended to the plain the panorama is even more wide for the castle stands, now, up on its rock, shadowed, implacable, black with the morning sun behind it, or towards evening mellowing to a sweet silver-grey—a proud old warrior's held-high head—the last to bow to the forces of Oliver Cromwell.

But the first problem for the golfer is to keep his head down and not to admire the scenery.

Harlech is in many ways like a sweet, feminine Hoylake. It, too, is mostly on the flat, but with an exquisite caprice disappears for its last four holes into the heart of the dunes.

There is enough room for drives not entirely straight, but small cousins of the Westward Ho! rushes stand about the links to emphasise that here is an old, perhaps old-fashioned, links where luck has not yet been eliminated. There are two blind holes, also, and the greens lie mostly where Nature intended them to.

I think Harlech has a peculiarly happy, carefree atmosphere about it. It may be that the grandeur of its setting reduces golf to its right proportion. The dour and tight-lipped magnifier of mole-hills has real mountains to look at. "The line, here, at this hole, is *exactly* on Snowdon."

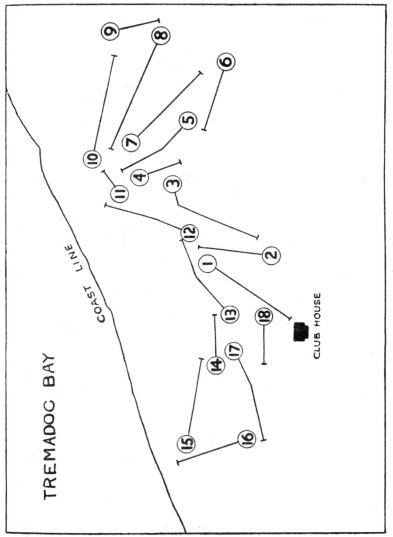

TREMADOC BAY

COAST LINE

CLUB HOUSE

HARLECH—Plan of the course

47

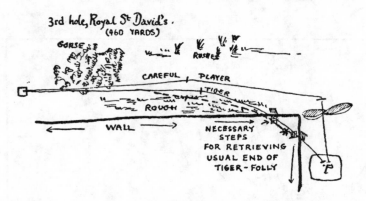

3rd hole, Royal St David's.
(460 YARDS)

GORSE

RUSHES

CAREFUL   PLAYER

TIGER

ROUGH

WALL

NECESSARY
STEPS
FOR RETRIEVING
USUAL END OF
TIGER - FOLLY

P

Harlech, once, even got the better of a Chancellor of the Exchequer who went out upon the links—typical—without paying his green fee!

Then there is the third hole—and this points the difference perfectly between Harlech and Hoylake. At this hole there is a wall all along the right-hand side of the rough—*not* so near as to be oppressive. As walls do, this takes in due time a right-angle turn; so does this delightful hole—the green is round the angle, too, and according to tee, wind, temperament, and skill you can tortoise round, or hare over the corner. This hole has an air of real golfing wit! One cannot be angry at it.

The story of the beginning of the links, also, has an air of fantasy. One day in the nineties a Mr. W. H. More, from the heights, saw a figure far below engaged in some strange form of exercise. He investigated and found a young man hurling a boomerang about. They fell into conversation and the young man said that his name was Harold Finch-Hatton, and that he had recently returned from Australia. A few days later, Mr. More observed him at some even stranger pursuit and perhaps a little gingerly went to investigate again. "Capital place for a golf links," said Finch-Hatton. "Come on, let's lay one out." Mr. More did not like somehow to admit that he knew absolutely nothing about golf—so the two went round placing tees and greens (Finch-Hatton said he was scratch at St. Andrews, whatever that meant); and so the course began, and More became secretary—a position he held with great skill and charm for forty years! I am sure the gay inconsequence of that beginning, and its happy continuance, still lingers. I would love to come upon that first aged and bibulous greenkeeper who was given an old hunting-pink coat as a badge of office and whose scarlet and stertorous recumbences were so frequent upon the links that a local rule was made—you could drop two clubs' lengths away without penalty.

The links does its best in June with purple patches of marsh orchis and ragged robin. I like to think they flower best in the little hollows which would have made ideal beds for those alcoholic lapses. In spring and early summer it is a wonderful place for the flora of marsh and sea-sand; the curlews come down from the mountains to nest and you can hear them making their wonderful accelerating bubble of a cry, almost like the cicada.

Where every prospect pleases
And only man is vile.

Bishop Heber, we know, wrote these words about Ceylon's isle—forcing the scansion out of the rough—and man was particularly vile in Ceylon because the good prelate's baggage had just been stolen. At Harlech, the height of villainy was Sunday golf, and it was not for a long time that the prospect of play was entertained at all—even now the nineteenth hole is exclusively soft—if you want to do a hole in one, do it on a Sunday.

Harlech is a 'minor' championship links; it is not epic golf but lyric golf of a first-rate quality—the Milton of *Comus*, not the Milton of *Paradise Lost*.

One does not feel claustrophobic behind the great sandhills—it's a long trek to the beach from the bottom of the castle cliff across the links to the holiday sea. Slightly testy parents and hot, tired children bear witness as they straggle across the twelfth fairway—in fact you do not see the sea and the long, safe stretch of the sands until the sixteenth tee; and then you turn your back on it and drive inland!

Harlech has one final twist—it ends with a short hole.

To return to the feminine simile, it is as if your love-suit had been going quite smoothly for thirteen holes—you propose on the thirteenth green—and there on the fourteenth tee the huge, sleeper-fanged Castle bunker rears up its question 'Yes or No'—

it's a blind spoon shot over—a carry all the way, for over the bunker is hummocky ground prickly with wild briar—but the hummocks may kick you in to a sunken green.

The 15th, a long two-shot hole, has a blind second over a rolling rise-and-fall-and-rise-again to a hidden cup of a green. It is a longish shot—and a good one will get you on—but a good lucky one will put you close—there's still hope. The 16th is a beautiful, difficult two-shot hole, again over a swell of narrow fairway, but to a green visible only if you hit a long straight drive.

At the 17th you must decide whether or not to carry a cross-bunker guarding the green.

All these four holes are a chapter of the agonies and renewed hopes of the lover, the last ploys of the beloved who knows in her heart that she will capitulate—but, by heaven, she is going to keep the ball rolling for as long as possible and see that it rolls pretty awkwardly at that. And then here is this nice friendly short 'yes' of an 18th to finish with—it has bunkers, of course, but not disastrous ones—and there's a *chance* to end with a 2—or even a 1.

Harlech is seven hours from London by train and there is "nothing to do" in the village; so it remains a tiny grey place on a hill-side, set in a scene of "mild magnificence", and unspoilt, as yet, by the developers and up-to-daters. I am not sure I should even say anything about Harlech at all—like that little restaurant in Soho where the cooking is superb—we tell only the chosen few of our friends who tell their chosen few. But then I am not sure that I *have* said anything about Harlech.

The late A. C. M. Croome wisely wrote, "No number of written words can convey an impression accurate in every detail of any course to the mind of a person who has never seen it."

Nor will a photograph really tell more than a menu.

Staying at Harlech is integrated with the links in that you cannot get lunch at the club house—only tea—so it is a question of returning to your hotel for lunch, or taking a packet of sandwiches with you.

There are three good hotels: *The Castle*, at the top, the *St. David's*, half-way up the hill, *The Queen's* on the level, nearest to the links. All are cognisant of the needs of golfers, such as drying clothes and being late for meals.

SCORE CARD

Hole	Yards	S.S.S.	Hole	Yards	S.S.S.
1	440	4	10	424	4
2	384	4	11	125	3
3	460	5	12	445	4
4	158	3	13	440	5
5	379	4	14	211	3
6	355	4	15	417	4
7	440	5	16	354	4
8	471	5	17	416	4
9	170	3	18	201	3
Out	3257	37	In	3033	34
			Out	3257	37
			Total	6290	71

LOCAL RULES

1. The following are out of bounds:
(*a*) Ground beyond the fence north of 1st tee.
(*b*) The road and ground north of the wall going to the 3rd hole as far as the gate near the 3rd green.
(*c*) Ground beyond the fence east of the 5th hole, military railway and road west of the 6th hole.
(*d*) Ground beyond wall and fence north of the 8th green.
(*e*) Railway fence and land to east.
(*f*) The putting green and club-house enclosure.
The penalty for out of bounds is loss of distance only.

2. A ball may be lifted from any hole made by a rabbit and dropped behind the same under penalty of one stroke, but if lifted from a bunker it must be dropped in the bunker not nearer the hole.

3. All drainage ditches are recognised water hazards. A ball lying in a ditch running parallel to the line of the hole at the 6th and 10th hole may be dropped as near as possible to the ditch not nearer the hole instead of behind.

4. A ball played on to a green other than the one being played to must be lifted and dropped not nearer the hole without penalty.

5. *Water Supply Pits.*—A ball lying within two clubs' length may be lifted and dropped without penalty as near as is possible to where the ball was lying but not nearer the hole.

6. *Pathway Leading to the Beach across the 13th Fairway.*—A ball lying on this pathway or within two clubs' lengths thereof may be lifted and dropped without penalty, the player when dropping the ball keeping the spot where the ball lay between himself and the hole.

HOYLAKE
Royal Liverpool

———◇———

THE links of the Royal Liverpool Golf Club is reckoned by everybody to be one of the finest tests of golf in the world. It is depressing to find on seeing it for the first time that it is utterly flat and dreary to look at, and for all the infinite subtleties to be discovered it remains rather formidably unattractive. It is, nowadays, not aesthetically improved by its two fringes of commodious, capacious, but architecturally deplorable villas whence commuters in bowler hats and with brief-cases shuttle to Liverpool.

A visit to Hoylake is rather like one's first visit to the Athenæum Club. Are these curious and shapeless old gentlemen, bumping and boring round, really the cream of the nation's intellect, carrying each in his own head Wisdom, Knowledge, Infinite Subtlety? Hoylake reminds me inevitably of them; long, slow, inexorable, and *right*. When Professor A. says that there were *No* ninth-century-B.C. spoons; there were, you know, NONE, not a single one—so off the very first tee at Hoylake the first hole dogmatically says: "I am right—you see, you thought you could take liberties with me; no; I am Professor Golf-Par. You missed that four-yarder? but, my dear fellow, there is something faulty in your putting, my greens are perfect." "But...?" "'Perfect,' I said."

The low, artificial two-foot-high banks are a feature of the links; they are called 'cops' and run along the edge of fairways. All the holes have names: 'the Dun', 'the Dowie', etc.; the 4th is called 'the Cop'. But here there is no cop visible from the usual tees and it is the easiest hole on the course—a typical don's high-table joke. The innumerable out-of-bounds—there are eight—are also like those sharp salty felisities[1] and ripostes on the high table whereby the thrusting Junior Fellows are put in their places. The very making of these cruel, artificial cops on this 'natural' seaside area is typical of Hoylake. Like those compulsory questions in

---

[1] *felis*, a cat.

exams—you have got to take notice of them, do them, and then ignore them so that you can get on with what you *do* know. Apart from the cops there is an air of the 'wide open spaces'— the area of the links is large, open, bare, agoraphobic: and the wind's paradise, the "haystack and roof-levelling wind".

Hoylake shares with bicycling the strange fact that whichever way you turn, the wind is plumb against, or at any rate unhelpful, across, or only behind when it is downhill, and you don't, anyway (e.g. the 13th), want it to be.

No, once on this Hoylake links, there is no means of avoiding prosecuting counsel's questions. It is a golfing cross-examination which will reveal and work upon every flaw in your golfing technique. It is at Hoylake that all golfing dentists should be forced to take their holidays. Hoylake probes relentlessly, finds the soft spot, and reaches for the drill.

Let us look carefully at the first hole. It is doglegged to the right, round the right angle of two cops: it needs a very long and brave drive to carry the corner. There is plenty of room to the left, and an average stroke will reach the corner, but it is quite easy to go out of bounds. You are left then with a perfectly simple second to the green. But all along the right runs the cop, its mean lowness is an open insult, and along its inside edge is a trough of sand. It is unpardonable but horribly easy to put your second out of bounds, as well as your first.

The second hole takes you towards the villa-tudordom road, and though a certain latitude may be allowed from the tee the approach must be perfect, for the green wears, like a dowager, a collar of precious bunkers: only a high straight pitch-and-stop will do.

There's a cop along the left of the long 3rd and no visible cop at the short 4th called, as we have seen, 'The Cop'. The fourth tee is right in the middle of the links, and is a good place to survey it from. You are, roughly, facing the line of dunes along the shore and you have the club house at your back. Before you, both left and right, is the most attractive part of the links. The holes from the 5th to the 13th are before you, and these holes constitute the more gentle element of the links. They are, to my mind, the best holes also.

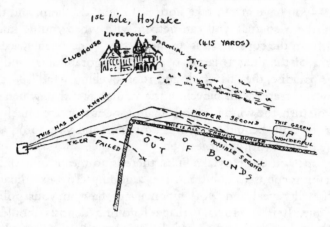

Now turn inland and face towards the Royal Hotel. There is the famous Hoylake finish; flat, long, grinding, and inexorable; to be feared and admired—rather like the finale of Sibelius's Third Symphony: a long, slow winding-up, a steady accumulation and accretion.

If one were to divide Hoylake into the movements of a symphony one would go like this, I think:

1st Movement	Nos.	1–5
2nd Movement (*andante*)		6–12
3rd Movement (*scherzo*)		13
4th Movement		14–18

I would begin my second movement at No. 6, 'The Briars', because there one bold stroke from the tee, across a high out-of-bounds corner jutting from the left, takes you into the sea-zone; I would begin it there also because of the slow, steady balance of the holes: 4, 3, 5, 4, 4, 3, 4 they go, though you are not likely to score them perfectly. This is a gentle contemplative passage, not exactly lyrical—as, for instance, the slow movement of Beethoven's Pastoral is not deeply grievous, but a slow, flowing, *legato* passage shot through with hints, or with dramatic innuendoes of tragedy. There is the seventh hole, a great short hole, 'The Dowie'. Another cop crawls sulkily along the left edge of the green, enticing the ball to lip over into outlawry. The green is beautifully modelled and guarded without bunkers, and the ideal shot is a draw just wide enough to turn in and die on to the right-hand side of the green—but a shade too much and out you go.

The 8th undulates up to the far end of the links, and from the ninth tee one sees the whole stretch of the estuary sands and the Welsh coast across the Dee. It is a very pleasant view indeed. Along the sea-dunes in their season bloom thousands of wild briar-roses. They are small plants which make patches of rough along the left, and they give out a wonderfully sweet, pure scent when in flower, and this compounded with a warm western sea-breeze is sheerly magical and restorative to the worn golfer. Of course, if you get among these myriad white eyes your ball becomes a rose, the roses a thousand balls.

Here, farthest away from the asphalt roads of Hoylake, is the place, in June, looking for your ball among the roses, to con-sider the beliefs of your life and what your monument will be.

Wild flowers on golf links are either weeds or hazards. The roses have a very small practical golfing function and are spared; inland the weed-killers have been at their puritan work in rough as well as fairway. Of course, it is right and proper that they should; but Hoylake is so vast and flat that these austere golfing acres could do with a little innocent decoration. Hoylake is Puritan, yes: a three-hour sermon in a gaunt building, all white-washed walls and black-clad sinners, or a three-hours round this gloomy, marvellous links, there's not much difference. It's Hell-fire or humble self-surrender to a God who will not tolerate a frivolous stroke, or laughter on the greens. Is golf a game at all, or a form of self-denial, or masochism? Remember that C. E. Jung went one better than Freud and discovered a whole rich vein of sexual symbolism in this game. I am not suggesting that regular players at Hoylake should be psycho-analysed, but I am sure the psycho-analyst should play here also—in combat with the dentist, if possible. I would really like to see a bishop, a dentist, a psycho-analyst, and a professional politician play a series of four-somes round Hoylake. You see, Hoylake is quietly bringing out the venom in me even in meditation upon its most lyrical and pleasant spot: out with it, then, I would like to see them *suffer*! Let us play the ninth hole, which is easy and old-fashioned, into a

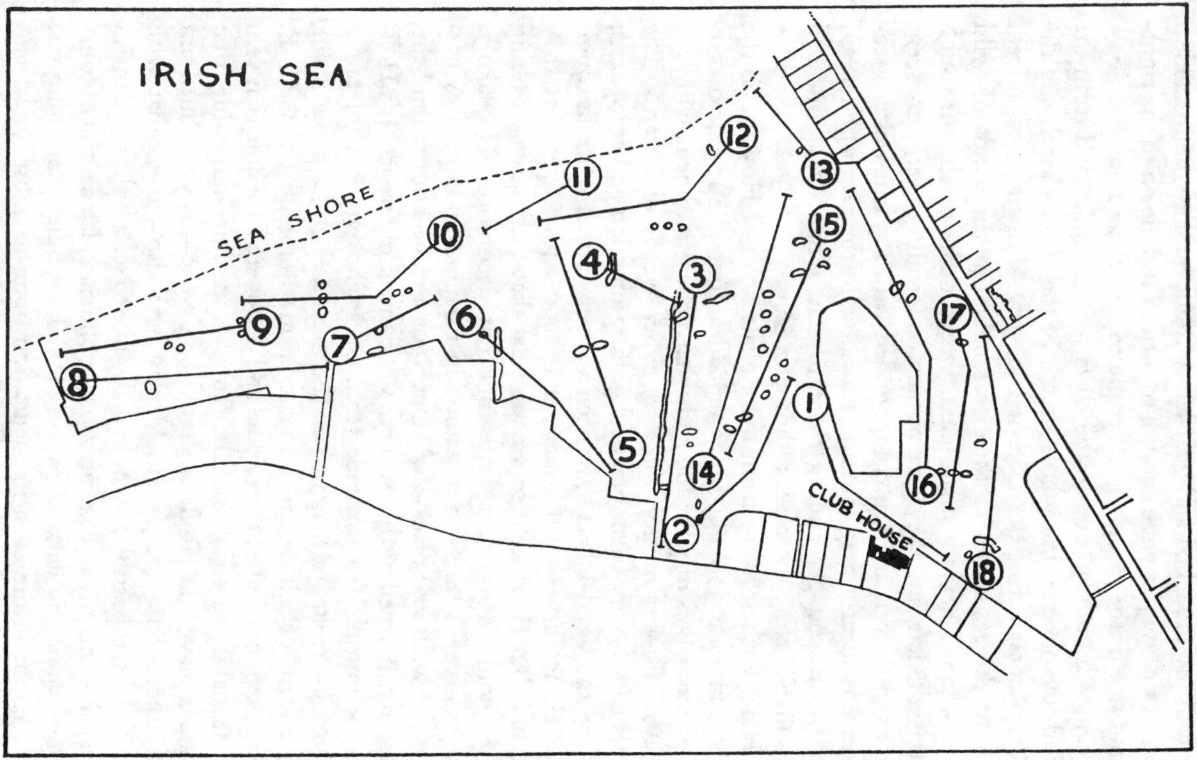

IRISH SEA
SEA SHORE
CLUB HOUSE
1
2
3
4
5
6
7
8
9
10
11
12
13
14
15
16
17
18

HOYLAKE—Plan of the course

punch-bowl of a green. The 10th, 11th, and 12th are beautiful, excellent golf holes.

And the short, wicked 13th, cocking a snook inland like 'a little vulgar boy', at the whole cold grind to come, is exactly like the *scherzo* of a symphony: gay, jiggety, tricky, witty, deplorable perhaps, but what a relief!

Then the finale begins. The 14th is called the 'Field', rightly, and is a gruelling flat slog along: the 15th brings you back again almost parallel. Both these holes are open and free.

The 16th is doglegged to the right over the cop-made corner of the rectangular practice field, and more 5's are taken here than 4's, even in bounds. The 'Royal' goes towards the Royal Hotel, just across the road from the green, which lies at an awkward angle to the road, like a mat just askew from the hearth. You can get to the green in 2, or be in the road in 2, or play short. The Royal Hotel, a late-eighteenth-century barracky building—but the one piece of genuine architecture for miles—was built for the bathing craze of the period, fell into desuetude and revived as a golfers' hotel in the seventies. It was then owned by the great John Ball's grandfather.

The 18th, like the 2nd, has a necklace of bunkers. It is called the 'Stand', for this is where the Liverpool Hunt Club had their race-course, and it is on this inland half of the links that golf was begun in 1869.

Hoylake is a tough, epic links. Like one of those classics of literature which one is always being recommended to read—"You won't really enjoy it, but you *must* read it, it is an experience you will never forget . . . and it is beautifully written."

You cannot just walk into Hoylake any more than you can walk into the Athenæum and ask for a half of bitter. You must be introduced by a real live member: in person, or by letter. Decorum must be observed. Club servants in livery pad about silently and look melancholy, as good club servants always must, in order that the members may feel the happier for seeing them.

When you have played you will be asked, "What do you think of the greens?" You will notice a sudden tension in the air. Hoylake has been waiting since 1869 for somebody to say '. . .', but you will say, "Wonderful". Everybody will relax—and you may go, now.

HOYLAKE

Hole	Name	Length	S.S.S.	Hole	Name	Length	S.S.S.
1	Course	415	5	10	Dee	410	4
2	Road	366	4	11	Alps	193	3
3	Long	455	5	12	Hilbre	401	4
4	Cop	158	3	13	Rushes	160	3
5	Telegraph	418	4	14	Field	486	5
6	Briars	383	4	15	Lake	443	5
7	Dowie	200	3	16	Dun	532	5
8	Far	482	5	17	Royal	394	4
9	Punchbowl	393	4	18	Stand	408	4
	Out	3270	37		In	3427	37
					Out	3270	37
					Total	6697	74

N.B.—The Standard Scratch Score would be made up as shown, but there is not an official bogey for the course.

LOCAL RULES

1. If a ball lodge in a rabbit hole or scrape on any part of the course except the putting green, it must be dealt with under the Rules of Golf. If a ball lodge in a rabbit hole or scrape on the putting green (Definition 27), it may be lifted, without penalty, and placed clear of the scrape, but not nearer the hole.

2. If a ball lie on any ground specially prepared for putting, other than that of the hole which is being played, it shall be lifted and dropped without penalty not less than two or more than three clubs' length from the edge of such prepared ground and in the direction of the fairway of the hole being played, but not nearer the hole. If a hazard interfere with the dropping of the ball or the stance of the player, the ball shall be dropped not more than two clubs' length clear of such hazard in the direction of the fairway of the hole being played but not nearer the hole.

3. Rushes and grass-bottomed ditches are not hazards, but in casual water in such a ditch the ball may be lifted and dropped in the ditch without penalty or outside with the loss of one stroke but not nearer the hole in either case.

Note.—A ball lying in or beyond the trenches cut in the top of the cops is out of bounds.

HUNSTANTON

Hunst'on the ancestral home of the le Stranges
Dates back to far away,
Hunstanton stands as evidence of changes
Of yesterday.

Before the time when ticket clerk and porter
And cheap excursion came
No one preferred Hunstanton to the shorter
And sweeter name. . . .

THAT seems to settle the question of the name, though for the purposes of the Post Office (both 'gram and 'phone) the longer and less sweet pronunciation is necessary.

Hunstanton was founded in March 1891. And the Club's first president, Hamon le Strange, supported the venture to . . . "the magnificent extent of £30! Think of that, ye golfing experts," wrote J. C. Morgan Brown in 1912 on the club's coming of age, "who reckon that a sum of £100 per hole ought to be allowed as the minimum cost of laying out a new course."

Comparative costs are always enthralling, particularly now that the Chancellor's system of national handicapping is so severe. The course was extended from nine to eighteen holes for the additional cost of £25, in the early years of the century!

Natural golfing country among sandhills is always rough and ready, so to speak, and Fernie would bind himself to stay only six weeks to lay out the original nine holes. "A drive and thirteen niblicks," noted an early visitor. Incidentally, these lucky early visitors were able, as late as 1914, to reach Hunstanton by train in under two and a half hours from London, but modern locomotive progress has stopped that sort of rot, and the journey now takes nearly four hours, including some fascinating shunting at Ely and King's Lynn.

59

Early days at Hunstanton must have been exciting. The first entry in the competition book notes laconically . . . "the above were the scores under 100" (May 2nd, 1892). But the great Vardon and Herd played an exhibition match in 1896, Vardon doing 75, 73 and Herd 70, 77. Taylor did a 73 in 1903.

James Braid contented himself—if not the members—by suggesting the addition of some sixty new bunkers to the course.

> *Whether 'tis nobler for a club to suffer*
> *Under the rather thinly veiled suggestion*
> *That she too gladly tolerates the duffer*
> *Or by a scheme of neatly planned obstruction . . .*
> *By right-and-left-placed pitfalls to betray*
> *And bring about the justly earned destruction . . .*

a lyrical member commented soon after his visit.

Seaside golf, of its nature, has always suffered from a lack of fresh water and consequently in the early days, before piped water was available, greens were placed in cups and hollows in the dunes, which made approaching easy and pleasant. The perching of greens on watered heights has made a difference. This is certainly true at Hunstanton, where the present lay-out dates essentially from 1925 and emanates from the subtle mind of J. G. Sherlock, himself a master of the short game—indeed a very fine golfer, in all respects.

Looking north from the club-house window the sea is to your left and the links stretches out like Prince of Wales's feathers, if you can imagine the central feather as a long duney ridge and the first nine holes inland to the right, the second nine to the left and seaward. This central ridge makes a wonderful natural grandstand, and by moving up and down it you can see the play at nearly every hole. What is curious is how immediately the land changes its character. Here is the links "between the desert and the sown", and looking inland, first there is a lush, pastoral, marshy lot of fields, then rising arable ground. One can hardly imagine the sea. Dividing the links from the countryside flows the river Hun, "shorn and parcelled" between straight, built-up banks, and it may serve one well as a symbol of the first few holes, for one does get a shut-in feeling from these also.

Each man must feel,
And some a good deal,
Of awe for our fateful first bunker.

Sixty-fives and *Penfolds* have reduced its awesomeness since the days when *Haskells* and *Colonels* and *Why-Nots*, like early aeroplanes, could only just make it, but this first bunker to be carried from the tee has a fine amplitude, a largesse of sand.

But once over it you are on the landward side, and bearing slightly inland from the central backbone, and the first five holes are more like seaside visitors than real inhabitants. They are good visitors; they wear the right clothes and behave with decorum, yet, so to speak, when they strip for the sea they shiver, or laugh too heartily, and their arms and legs are white. Do not imagine, however, that they are easy. Their *character* may be inland but their *nature* is seaside, like a fisherman's children who have gone to make money in the midlands.

The 2nd is as long as an office Friday and as hard to get through without trouble, and the 3rd is that Saturday morning the juniors sit through, knowing the boss isn't in, and at 11.30 *in he walks*, the embodiment of the easy par 4 you thought you had got away with—but now . . .

So you dash for the short 4th, like your precious Saturday afternoon. All round the green are pot-bunkers, hangovers from the week—you just miss the train—I mean the green, but never mind, a 4 will do—and up on to the ridge for the 5th tee—there's the sea! and the second nine, opening out and then—you drive away inland again, down on to a wide, flat fairway and play your second through a gap in a grassy bank on to a flat green. If ever a hole was like a provincial Sunday it is the 5th! I do not mean that these first five holes are not good golf holes: the 2nd—in particular—is a fine test of hitting—but that in comparison with what is to come they are relatively uninspiring. But from the sixth tee onwards Hunstanton is a really first-class, an exciting and various test of golf and it has one hole which is supreme and unique—but to return to the sixth tee: you look up the slope, the crest of the dune ridge,

61

HUNSTANTON—Plan of the course

NORTH SEA

CLUB HOUSE

and there is the green, a small sloping table with precipitous falls on either side, though the right-hand crater is over a deceiving lip.

Does the road lead uphill all the way?
Yes, to the very end.

After a drive up the nursery slopes, the ground rises at a steep pitch—and needs a steep pitch shot. Once on the green, putting from anywhere save directly below the hole will have a strong and persistent borrow. Four putts could easily be taken. The next hole is a short hole, and the green is perched between the twin crests of dune which end the long ridge: in between tee and green is a cavernous crater and if you fall short you will need a shot as perpendicular as a lark to soar up singing and fall mute and satisfied on the green. Nothing but a straight all-carrying shot will do. The long 8th goes out to the very end of the links and the 9th returns skirting the seaward end of the ridge to a green directly below the sixth green and seventh tee.

My own preference is for the second nine, which I think compares well with any other nine championship holes you may like to put against it; though it may be a little too short for perfection and it has a blind shot in it such as nowadays is found Victorian and unamusing. Having said that, let us come to the 13th. Let no iconoclast dare come near with talk of alteration. Hunstanton has in this hole a pure and original poem of a hole; as well alter this, as ask Sir Alfred Munnings to paint out the Mona Lisa's smile and substitute a horse-laugh.

The tee, inland, faces at right angles to the central ridge, and upon the top, and just over the top, of this is a large handkerchief of fairway and here you must place your drive, towards the left side; breast the slope and stand then with a wonder and a wild surmise! For the fairway just stops dead at the bottom of the slope. Where is the green? Look seaward and, a little left, over a flat but undulant tract of little rushy, sandy hillocks, anything but Pacific, and there just beyond them, a hundred and fifty yards away in all, is the green! There is no approach to this save by air. The green lies like one of those little lost civilisations in some valley encircled by impassable mountains. Here these intervening mountains are perfectly passable though slowly and perhaps with pain. This second shot—usually it is up into the wind—needs really accurate striking: the green lies just at the angle to take a slightly cut-up shot coming in from the left and your ball, if it lands on, will stay on: if it lands short it will stay short. I know of no other hole that has its rough after its fairway quite like this; no other hole that calls for quite such skilled and controlled strokes; nor looks simply so 'right' and fascinating. I take this to be one of the greatest two-shot holes in golf. It has always struck me as strange that it is *direction*, rather than *length*, that is the more difficult thing to judge and to control in golf: at this hole the emphasis, in both shots, is on an exact judgement of length; for the short-handicap long-hitter will find himself in difficulty if, only just off the line to the right, he goes too far: and I'm afraid this is a sheerly intolerant hole for the long-handicap short-hitter; he will be in trouble with his second, and hope thereafter for luck.

13th hole, Hunstanton
rough cross-section
(390 YARDS)

We have left, still, the 15th, the valley hole, deep and secret on the lee-side of the dune, sheltered from the wind and altogether enchanting; the 16th, a beautiful longish one-shotter; and a new finish.

One used to cross over the ridge to the 17th, walk a long way inland to the 18th tee and play up towards the club house with the first hole on the right. Now both 17th and 18th keep to the sea-side and make an extremely testing and exciting finish.

Hunstanton is one of those few links of real class which is also kind to the average player, not *"incompossible"*: it is not *too* long, nor *too* difficult to enjoy, and if it is not crowded—ought I to say this?—there are some excellent short-cuts if you don't want to play a full round. The gentle slope of the Wash provides a vast beach for family bathing, paddling, and castle-making, and along at New Hunstanton there is a chalk-cliff, and odd rock-pools.

Within easy reach, too, is its neighbour and rival for favour in golfing argument, Brancaster, now happily reclaimed from an inrush of warlike waters.

> Yes, Hunston in one little word embraces
> The love of shining sands,
> Of rock and pool and all the winning graces
> Of Norfolk strands. . . .

HUNSTANTON

SCORE CARD

Hole	Yards	S.S.S.	Hole	Yards	S.S.S.
1	338	4	10	375	4
2	541	5	11	446	4
3	438	4	12	359	4
4	158	3	13	390	4
5	423	4	14	225	3
6	332	4	15	457	5
7	164	3	16	188	3
8	493	5	17	454	5
9	520	5	18	405	4
Out	3407	37	In	3299	36
			Out	3407	37
			Total	6706	73

LOCAL RULES

1. *Out of bounds:*
(a) The River Hun.
(b) On the right of the 8th hole a ball lying in or beyond the ditch short of the road, or the wire fence and beyond it the ditch, over the road.
(c) A ball lying over the fence on the right of the 18th hole.

2. A ball played on to any putting green other than that of the hole which is being played must be lifted and dropped off the green, the player keeping the spot from which the ball was lifted between himself and the hole, or played with a putter.

3. At the 8th hole a ball lying in the trenches, or on that part of the roadway between the trenches or within two clubs' length of the trenches on either side, may be lifted and dropped behind without penalty.

4. A ball lying in a rabbit scrape, anywhere on the course except in a bunker, may be lifted and dropped immediately behind the scrape without penalty, provided that a club placed over the scrape does not touch the ball.

66

LITTLE ASTON

THIS is the kind of golf course which an eighteenth-century English gentleman would have approved. It is, of course, laid out in the parkland which belonged to Little Aston Hall; and its lay-out is neat, formal, yet imaginative. It was the work of Harry Vardon in 1908. Later corrections in proof were made by H. S. Colt, but the present excellence of the course—its long, steady trend to maturity—is the work of Mark Lewis, who came to the club as professional in 1909 and has only just retired from active service after forty years. An excellent and typical feature of the club—which exemplifies the happy relationship—is that the professional's shop opens directly off the men's dressing-room; and how many hopeful expeditions must have gone out with Mr. Lewis's benevolent advice, to return broken and defeated, craving comfort—nor was it easy to blame it on one's clubs, under the eye of their maker! Mr. Lewis is an expert club-maker, and since that beautiful golfer C. H. Ward came into partnership with him one can see many members performing their fruitless evolutions on the greens with faithful replicas of Ward's putter—such is the power of magic in this age of science and reason.

The greens of Little Aston are large, beautifully kept, and exceedingly cunning. They are such greens as Professor Einstein would delight to putt on—for there is no such thing as a straight line however, superficially, it may appear so. The slightest of inclines, the subtlest, finest of borrows and curling declivities bear the ball away to touch the hole like a tangential arc. These greens are nightmare billiard tables—none more so than the 17th, which is a rectangular tableland with bunkers all round it like pockets, and the difficulties of pitching on it are nicely emphasised by the pretty waterlilied lake of the Hall which is away to its left—too far to the left, surely, to pull one's approach into? It has often been done!

As you stand upon the club-house terrace you face westward, and look beyond the park to a rising countryside of pasture; it is impossible to believe you are only a few miles from the vast industrial sprawl of Birmingham. The whole place is so peacefully sylvan that you feel, "I mustn't tell too many people about this; I must keep it to myself, or the peace will be broken", and as a matter of fact it is extremely difficult to find the Little Aston Golf Club, at all! For it lies behind a screen of large mansions each 'standing in its own grounds', well-timbered, rhododendroned, and beshrubbed. You turn into what looks like somebody's private approach, and timidly pushing ahead and prepared to run up a white flag at the slightest hint of danger, you penetrate deep into this luscious interior, turn to the left, pass a pillar-box under a tree and there you are in the car-park at the back of the club house. Even having dared so far it is difficult to get *into* the club house. But persevere: facing the building, bear round it to the left and you will find the professional's shop, like an Ellis Island friendly to the immigrant. Once in you will be welcome, and the course will welcome you also.

But before you play—in order quite to break your putting nerve—have a turn round the putting course, just in front of the terrace. This is no ordinary putting course, flat and clockwise. If you can imagine a jigsaw puzzle of which some of the pieces are curiously curving beds of heather and the other pieces which fit into them are grass-green, you may get some idea of this amusing and tantalising instrument of torture. Apart from winding among heather beds, the holes undulate and wriggle and wallow. If you can get round in level 2's you will almost certainly take three putts on every green of the course proper; if you start taking 3's, or even 4's, or running off the pretty into the heather in a carefree way, thinking "I won't spoil my touch on *this*", well, . . . I won't say. . . .

The most obvious feature to catch the eye from the terrace is the long magnificent avenue that is drawn up all along one side of the course. We will walk its length like an inspecting general, along the 3rd, 4th, and 8th which could be played as one gigantically long hole, able to be reached, I suppose, with a drive, four full brassie shots, and a pitch.

These are three holes at which a hooked tee shot, unless you are lucky enough to ricochet, is a disaster. There is plenty of room at

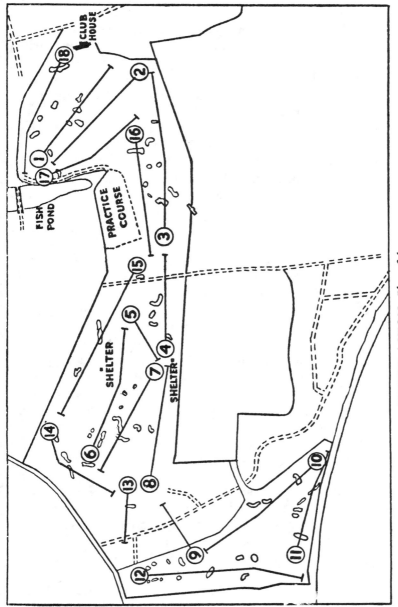

LITTLE ASTON—Plan of the course

Little Aston, though certain strategic trees have been left standing about looking innocently picturesque, like those pretty ignorant-of-golf spectators who come to be admired, but are obstinately deaf and immobile when standing in the line of play. "But I thought they hit it down the *middle* of the fairground, dear." "The fairway? Not always. You were right on his line there." "Sounds like a wrong number." "Oh, well. . . ."

The fairways are, to a seaside golfer, almost too perfect. The ball sits up and ogles one too blatantly for words.

The difference between seaside and inland golf could not be better pointed than here. To retain the eighteenth-century analogy, here is Nature obedient to Man, who has made an artificial pattern, and imposed a logical order upon the wild and unruly. Many inland courses look 'wrong' in their environment, as if they had been spread from a tube upon something else and could be scraped off to disclose what was originally there. The first-rate park course, however, has its own integrity. It looks as if it *ought* to be there; a natural adjunct of man's civilised life. Little Aston looks quite natural and right: the artifice of man has gone full circle here; and, to ram this particular point home to our attention, three of the holes, the 10th, 11th, and 12th, escape from the park; the 10th on to a moorlandy, heathy zone which before Little Aston Park was made must have been the aboriginal countryside; and the 11th and 12th on to fields also previously claimed from open heath. These three holes have slightly the air of a poor but worthy relation who has been settled, on a small pension, just outside the great lord's gates (and secretly hopes for something in the will), and they are in process of 'improvement'.

To get to these three holes there are two excellent gates. The short 9th, whose green is invitingly wide, outside the trees through which the tee shot must be carved, is into the prevailing south-west wind and once the ball is free of its arboreal screen any impurities of striking, cut, or draw, will tell. The very short 13th re-entrance gate is a beautiful hole to a long green with an outstanding clump of trees a little forward from the wood, on the left, making you believe there is half the room there actually is. It is notable also that the two holes, the 8th preceding the exit and the 14th postsequential to the ingress, are the two best two-

14th hole, Little Aston.

(323 YARDS)

shot holes on the course. This 14th, doglegged right over a cross-bunker, is a particularly good hole, for the line, against all the outward and visible signs, is as conservative and down the left as possible, and the long cross-country hitter will find himself into or near or stymied by a peculiarly maddening tree. With all the fal-lal which goes on about stymies on the putting green it is interesting to speculate about natural stymies through the green. Putting is not intrinsically more important than driving; and though one's opponent does not leap ahead to plant the stymying tree, neither does he deliberately lay the stymying putt. Agreed also that it is possible to be stymied on every green and that it is impossible to find oneself behind a tree from every tee, yet it seems to me that the anti-stymyist, removing a natural hazard of the game and replacing it with an artificial convention, is doing a dangerous thing. He is interfering with 'the natural use of land', and recently a learned judge ruled that keeping three-quarters of a million bees in a small area was 'natural use of land' even though they attacked and killed the neighbour's goats and wounded his wife. One could find no better possible debating-place for the stymie than Little Aston, with its beautifully kept meretricious greens and its bank balance of fairway and rough; for this fairway and rough are like one's account, credit somehow topples over the line into the red, and that same figure 4 which looked so prosperous becomes minus 4—one cannot quite say how or why. Just the texture is different. You don't *lose* your ball or even have to hack it out very hard, but the rough is thick and woolly and claggy on the club like cold rice pudding: difficult to get rid of.

Little Aston is one of the few clubs where caddies, real caddies, and not human bag-porters, are still to be had, not too exorbitantly, and it is also an easy course for the mechanical-caddy.

One of the difficulties of visiting this charming and exceedingly good golf course is where to visit it from. On a golfing holiday there must be days when golf palls; but there are no architectural glories to detain one in Sutton Coldfield, the nearest town. It is best to stay at Lichfield, where Dr. Johnson was born; and whose observations upon golf, *vis-à-vis* the Scot and the Englishman, would have been worth preserving. Lichfield is a small country town with a beautiful and delicate cathedral, on any count worth a visit. South-west of Birmingham, Warwick and Stratford-upon-Avon are within a car's hour, and you could possibly combine Shakespeare and golf, muttering, if you like, "the course of true love never did run smooth". Little Aston is about as near contradicting that as any course you are likely to play on.

The club is old enough to keep the women in comparative purdah, but they are allowed at least half the dining-room and have their own and comfortable lounge. The food—to be ordered in advance, which means when you arrive—is excellent, and I cannot really imagine why I am not going to give detailed and meticulous directions how to get there, but, I think, as to Southwell Minster, the interested enthusiast will find his way there sooner or later and, without being extended to the utmost, will enjoy himself. Little Aston is in good taste and has a good taste.

LITTLE ASTON

SCORE CARD

Holes	Length	S.S.S.	Holes	Length	S.S.S.
1	382	4	10	463	5
2	439	4	11	382	4
3	500	5	12	482	5
4	329	4	13	148	3
5	159	3	14	323	4
6	427	4	15	548	5
7	368	4	16	413	4
8	392	4	17	361	4
9	179	3	18	386	4
Out	3175	35	In	3506	38
			Out	3175	35
			Total	6681	73

LOCAL RULES

(For Match and Stroke Play)

Competitors shall be governed by the St. Andrews Rules of Golf, subject to the following Local Rules

1. Any ball played on to a green other than that of the hole in play shall be lifted and dropped off the green not nearer the hole, and so that the line to the hole is not improved thereby.

2. Three- and four-ball matches must, on being overtaken, give way to a properly constituted match without request being made.

3. Any ball lodging in or outside any boundary fence or within the putting course or ditch surrounding is out of bounds.

4. *Practice Area.*—Players may practise from any of the five marked practice patches provided they do not play towards the following greens: 1, 2, 16, 17, or 18.

MOORTOWN

IF you stand on the first tee, a stranger, at Moortown you may reasonably wonder where this famous course *is*. You are looking down a sloping fairway, and away all down the left-hand side is a birchwood spinney to which the land falls. On the right, coming up over the rise is, obviously the 18th. Where is the rest?

The answer begins in 1903, when Mr. F. Lawson Brown took a holiday at Bridlington. While he was there he went over to see the Yorkshire Amateur Championship played at Ganton. Any golfer going to Ganton draws delighted breath, but Mr. Lawson Brown was not a golfer. What he saw was a strange game being played in beautiful surroundings. This is a significant and remarkable thing, for one of the pleasures of golf is its environment. Ganton set him a high standard—it is as if one's first introduction to music, having heard none whatever, were Beethoven's *Pastoral Symphony*; or having seen no drama, *A Midsummer Night's Dream*; or, in painting, the landscapes of *Corot* or *Constable*. Nothing afterwards must fall short of these standards.

So Mr. Lawson Brown returned to Leeds inspired by an aesthetic appreciation of golfing country: a man determined to find for Leeds the equivalent of what Ganton *looked like*! And, "curiouser and curiouser", he enlisted three other non-golfing musketeers in this remarkable quest to find the right and beautiful, the golfable place. This hunt must have been not unlike Lewis Carroll's *Hunting of the Snark*.

They sought it with thimbles, they sought it with care,
They pursued it with forks and hope. . . .

And finally they found it. Often in the months that followed they must have thought their Snark was a Boojum which caused those who saw it to

Softly and suddenly vanish away. . . .

But the pioneers persevered, and after eight months of huntings, meetings, and even enlisting the support of already-golfers, they were prepared.

I have said that from the first tee one can see very little—this land was in fact the last to join the club. It first began up on a heathery, boggy hill-side, full of stagnant pools, called Blackmoor. Blackmoor runs down northwards to a stream, and north of the stream on the other slope of the valley was farmland: and all this land is on the other side of the rectangular spinney to the west. Where they cut the first hole on the wild moor lie now the ninth–fourteenth holes. Their first hole is the present 14th—a gentle downhill beginning for these indomitable men who decided to lay out a beautiful course first, and then learn to play on it—beautifully, one hopes.

Luckily for them Dr. Alastair McKenzie, the golf architect, was in the district laying out Alwoodley—another course, incidentally, well worth a visit. He was co-opted, and adding his professional eye to their ardent amateur vision he realised that here was golfing country *par excellence*, and with Mr. Lawson Brown at the other end of the chain measured out nine holes on Blackmoor and its opposite pastoral slope. The whole of Blackmoor had to be drained—the ancient stone drains were cleared, rubble-drainage applied, and slowly the holes took shape. (Clubs were kept in a neighbouring farmer's barn.) Greens were *laid*. For an inland course this was a revolutionary change from the cut-out flat pocket-handkerchief variety. To design and lay out the equivalent of the rolling seaside green was a unique affair! As you putt on the present seventh green recall that people came from far and wide to see this eighth wonder of the golfing world. The excitement of those days is lost now to golf: what is to be the next step in golf-course design we do not know, unless it be radiated bunkers which keep the sand dry and at an even temperature.

I have kept you on the present first tee almost as long as it takes an American golfer to study the line of a six-inch putt. Now it is time to play round. Walking down the first fairway, you will at once find your feet treading a springy turf—almost the whole course is on good springy peat—and to say this is to remember

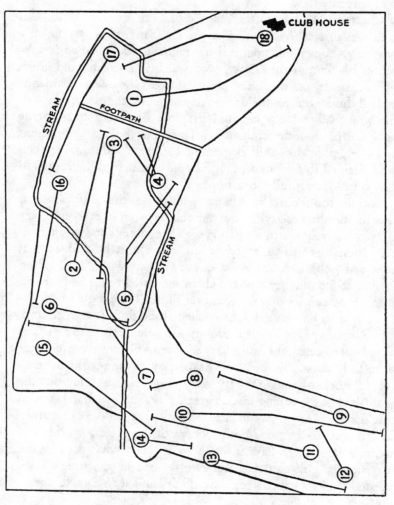

MOORTOWN—Plan of the course

that, as you approach the first green, and see to the right the seven-teenth fairway, you are on a peaty bottom: a bog where cattle were once lost and where the workers had to be *roped* together when the site was first cleared and drained. Through the corner of the spinney you walk to your first sight of what you imagine the whole course will be; a slight disappointment, perhaps. You drive westwards along a rather parky fairway: these were fields, you think, good lush grazing. Then upon the third tee turning right back, a completely new course seems to emerge. Driving over a constellation of bunkers, one sentinel fir-tree, rather Chinese-looking, guides you parallel to the second fairway yet urges you to look right rather than left along the whole northern vista of the birchwood, and with a little runnel of heather along the left edge of the fairway you are suddenly in heathery-heathy country like a Surrey course, but with what a difference!

The short 4th thrusts boldly right into the trees and the way, though clear, is knobbly with round, trimmed, birch-trees, half like some Elizabethan maze in a formal garden—but as one stands on the fifth tee to escape from the wood again, this formal-ity takes on a rather sinister air. The first 120 yards or so must be carried over this rounded, diseased-looking growth. It looks like a tank-trap, and is certainly a head-up trap. This 5th is a lovely hole. A draw round the corner of the wood (and two more sentinel firs stand to salute your drives) and then all along the left-hand side of the fairway silver birches watch you to the green like an attentive crowd. The 6th takes you north uphill on to the farm country again, and from the seventh tee you play the original 7th. It is a fine hole; a drive downhill, and doglegged to the right is that famous green. It is as you play your second that a real wide, windy moorland feeling, and view, open the lungs whether you know this is the 'old course' or not. Again, the scene shifts from birch to pure heather moor.

And at this moment, just as you feel free, comes a devilish short hole beckoning from a bower on the edge of the spinney like some beautiful witch. It is a ravishing hole to look at, an orchid of a hole; quite short, delightfully tempting, and needing a very, very good shot—three good shots to the bottom of the hole. And so to the 9th, where you can drive—blind—more to the

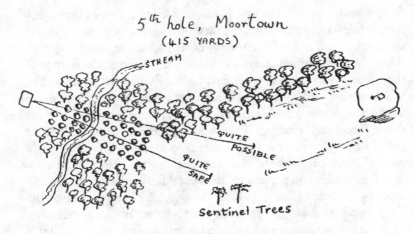

5th hole, Moortown
(415 YARDS)

STREAM

QUITE POSSIBLE

QUITE SAFE

Sentinel Trees

right than you think, and up you come on to Blackmoor—the original peat bog, full of those beer-coloured stagnant pools. What a metamorphosis! Here, now, is a real vintage-porty piece of golfing country; heathery rough, clumps of little birch-trees, narrow accuracy-demanding fairways, an up-and-down of the best kind of inland golf: 9th up to the old club house; long 10th right down; 11th up again, short 12th across the top, 13th down, with an ancient dry-stone wall all the way to your left—there for hundreds of years before golf began. Still downhill, and here you are on the 14th—the original 1st. Think of the *Ocobos* and *Haskells* and *Avon Fliers* despatched from here by short spoons, mid-irons, or light irons! Now it is a flick with a No. 5 or 6.

After the 14th you cross the valley bottom and up the hill-side, and the wildness has gone. You are back on the farmland. At the 16th you will find Sam King's bridge—three solid railway sleepers —which he caused to be removed in order to play from the bottom of the stream in a competition which he ultimately won! And so, over the bones of engulfed cattle and back up the rise, to the club house.

Moortown is a fascinating course, and unlike most inland courses it does cumulatively give one the impression of natural growth, though its three elements are not *quite* integrated. It has expanded rightly, and shrewdly, from its first impossible beginnings, and although the red-ribbon roofs of Alwoodley Lane spoil the view north-west and houses have crept all along the 17th, still the old creeper-covered foursquare farmhouse is on the hill behind the seventh tee to remind one what the view was like, when nothing was there but itself. In 1929 Moortown had its great moment, when England, against the odds, won the Ryder Cup. It has indeed been the scene of many great competitions, and will be. When you have played round with a card take a look in the dining-room at C. H. Ward's record 64—I do not recommend this before you go out unless you think you can better it. Nor, perhaps, is it likely to aid the digestion of the excellent meal you will get!

As you will realise when you have played round, the central spinney is roughly rectangular and the course goes three sides round it like three white squares contingent on one black square on a chessboard; and it uses the best country available. The site of Moortown was chosen with courage and vision. To point the difference, just north of Moortown over the other side of the farm-hill is Sand Moor, a course well worth visiting also, being of quite another character. It is a downland course of swoops and hollows, vistas and declivities, and the basic soil is clay. As everyone knows, golf is a game dependent on its ground, although the ball covers the distance of the course, or should do, mostly in the air. But, as with aeroplanes, the landings and take-offs are all-important. On the peat at Moortown you crash by your own failure.

MOORTOWN

SCORE CARD

Hole	Length	S.S.S.	Hole	Length	S.S.S.
1	500	5	10	586	5
2	415	4	11	445	5
3	450	5	12	170	3
4	183	3	13	425	4
5	415	4	14	146	3
6	224	4	15	390	4
7	429	4	16	425	4
8	162	3	17	360	4
9	380	4	18	410	4
Out	3158	36	In	3357	36
			Out	3158	36
			Total	6515	72

LOCAL RULES

1. *Out of Bounds:*
   (*a*) Over the wall at the 8th, 9th, 12th, and 13th.
   (*b*) Over the wall and over the paddock at the 14th.
   (*c*) Left of the paddock at the 15th, and left of the fence at the 16th, 17th, and 18th.

2. A ball lying on a green other than that in play must be lifted and dropped on the nearest part of the course not nearer the hole.

Note.—All positions where players may lift and drop without penalty are indicated by a notice.

MUIRFIELD

———————◆———————

North from Edina eight furlongs or more
Lies that famed field, on Fortha's sounding shore;
Here Caledonia's chiefs for health resort,
Confirm their sinews in the manly sport.
Macdonald and unmatched Dalrymple ply
Their pond'rous weapons and the greens defy;
Rattray for skill and Crosse for length renowned,
Stuart and Leslie beat the sandy ground. . . .
THOMAS MATHISON from *The Goff,* 1743

THE poet was a lawyer's clerk, and himself a golfer; obviously he knew these Caledonian chiefs by sight and style of play: but he was not one of the select band of "Gentleman Golfers" who met at Mrs. Clephan's tavern on play-days at Leith and drank deeply of claret after their games. These gentle.nen golfers were a 'club', that is, a group in the habit of meeting together, well before 1744. We know this, since they had more than once applied to the City Fathers for recognition before that date, and in 1744 the 'Good Town' recognised them as a worthy body, and presented a Silver Club to be played for—cannily providing that no expense should be chargeable to the Town save the advertisement of the competition the day before. This was bravely done through the streets with crier and 'tuck of drum'.

The winner was to be deemed "Captain of the Golf" and to have absolute jurisdiction in all golfing matters whilst he was the holder. "Rattray, for skill . . . renowned," was the first winner.

Whatever its intentions, the competition for the Silver Club was a closed event, confined to the Gentlemen Golfers (poets were not considered gentlemen, then). In order to hold a competition you must have rules, and the Gentlemen Golfers had rules—*the oldest rules in the whole game*—and the original copy of them, signed by John Rattray, hangs in the club house at Muirfield:

1. *You must tee your ball within a club's length of the hole.*

2. *Your tee must be upon the ground.*

3. *You are not to change the ball which you strike off the tee.*

4. *You are not to remove Stones, Bones, or any Break-Club, for the sake of playing your ball. Except upon the fair green and that only within a club's length of your ball.*

5. *If your ball comes among Watter, or any Wattery filth, you are at liberty to take out your ball and bringing it behind the hazard and teeing it, you may play it with any club and allow your adversary a stroke, for so getting out your ball.*

6. *If your balls be found anywhere touching one another you are to lift the first ball, till you play the last.*

7. *At Holling you are to play your ball honestly for the hole and not to play upon your opponent's ball not lying in your way to the hole.*

8. *If you shou'd lose your ball, by its being taken up, or any other way, you are to go back to the spot, where you struck last, and drop another ball and allow your adversary a stroke for the misfortune.*

9. *No man at Holling his ball is to be allowed to mark his way to the hole with his club or anything else.*

10. *If a ball be stopped by any person, Horse, Dog, or anything else the ball so stopped must be played where it lies.*

11. *If you draw your club to strike and proceed so far in the stroke as to be bringing down your club; if then your club shall break, in any way, it is to be accounted a stroke.*

12. *He whose ball lies furthest from the hole is obliged to play first.*

13. *Neither trench, ditch or Dyke made for the preservation of the Links, nor the Scholar's Holes nor the Soldier's Lines shall be accounted as a hazard but the ball is to be taken out, teed, and played with any iron club.*

JOHN RATTRAY.

These are the original rules of golf.

Ten years later, in 1754, these rules were copied almost verbatim by St. Andrews when their own inaugural competition was held. Just as certain prompts, notes, and stage directions have been incorporated in the text of Shakespeare to the confusion of scholars—such as "Enter tawyer with a trumpet"—for years nobody knew what a tawyer was—until it was discovered it was the name of the props. manager; so the St. Andrews copyist made nonsense by copying out all of Rule 13. What exactly the Scholar's Holes were, or even the Soldier's Lines, nobody knows, but that they were peculiar to the Leith Links is certain.

Competitors at St. Andrews must have been extremely puzzled! I think it a pity these mysterious terms did not somehow become part of the game, like the terms in cribbage. Certainly, many golfers nowadays who make it a practice to tee up on the fairway should know this rule and claim to have been in a Scholar's Hole —it would give their malpractices a tremendous air of tradition and rectitude.

Recently, in *The Times*, there was the challenging phrase, "Chess is the only game at which it is impossible to cheat"—a sobering thought. Already in 1744 observe rule 9! Had someone been scoring a deep groove with the point of his iron?

Rule 1. "You must tee your ball within a club's length of the hole" is a reminder that teeing grounds are a late innovation: till the 1890's you still played from hole to hole, and *did* tee up and drive from near the last hole—a practice which must have further roughened the putting surfaces!

There's bound always to be argument, but there is little doubt that the Honourable Company is the oldest *Club* in the game, and it retains to this day some features eminently worthy of emulation. Those early convivial evenings at Mrs. Clephan's inn, when club business was done and matches arranged, developed into Match Dinners. At these, with due ceremony and formal phrases from the Captain, matches—now nearly always thirty-six hole foursomes—are arranged and bets laid on the protagonists. The Bets Book has been kept since 1776. There's an enchanting entry for February 9th, 1880—a single—"C. v. M. not played—C. funked." Did C. dare appear on the Links again?

"That famed field on Fortha's sounding shore" (I wish Mathison had had the courage to follow through his alliteration and write 'Fortha's frothy fringe'—it would have been a good tongue-tester to the old players, who, as Smollett records, took claret by the gallon). In his *Humphry Clinker* (1771) he has a racy description of the Leith Links:

Hard by, in the fields called the Links, the citizens of Edinburgh direct themselves at a game called golf, in which they use a curious kind of bats tipt with horn, and small elastic balls of leather, stuffed with feathers, rather less than tennis balls, but of a much harder consistence—these they strike with such force and dexterity from one hole to another that they will fly to an incredible distance. Of this diversion the Scots are so fond that when the weather will permit, you will see a multitude of all ranks, from the senator of justice to the lowest tradesman mingled together in their shirts, and following the balls with the utmost eagerness. Among others I was shown one particular set of golfers the youngest of whom was turned of four-score— They were all gentlemen of independent fortunes, who had amused themselves with this pastime for the best part of a century without ever having felt the least alarm from sickness or disgust, and they never went to bed without having each the best part of a gallon of claret in his belly. Such uninterrupted exercise cooperating with the keen air from the sea must without all doubt keep the appetite always on edge and steel the constitution against all the common attacks of distemper.

Some old bills tell the same story:

Sept 25 1791

Dinner	3.	o.
Claret	12.	o.
Port	2.	3.
Gin		4.
Porter & beer		8.
	18.	3.

Feb 20 1792

Dinner	2.	6.
Claret	19.	o.
Port	2.	3.
Sherry	3.	o.

These make interesting comparisons with 1950, but unluckily *quantities* are not recorded!

The course on Leith Links was five holes long, each hole being over four hundred yards and each having a name. Royal Blackheath, whose fabulous founding in 1608 is to be taken with a pinch of salt, had two holes—*the Thorntree* and *Braehead*—similarly named, showing perhaps that

Still the blood was strong, the heart was Highland

and that Scots, exiled South, were sentimental even in 1776. I have lingered over these early records because they are, like the traditions of William of Wykeham at Winchester, a living force at Muirfield to-day. Here is a place which has preserved the tra-

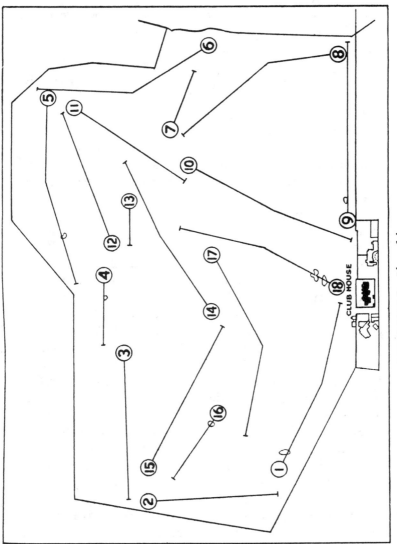

MUIRFIELD—Plan of the course

dition that "the manly sport is a courtly and graceful and enjoyable accomplishment".

Muirfield itself, like so many of the great links, belongs to the 1890's. The Honourable Company moved from Leith to Musselburgh in 1836—both Links being upon public land—and from Musselburgh to its own private and sequestered spot in 1891. "Just an auld water meadie," commented Andrew Kirkaldy, rudely.

J. H. Taylor was equally unimpressed.

Certainly it is as different from Westward Ho! as Bel Paese cheese is from Stilton.

Muirfield is not exactly seaside—it is above the sea. There are ridges of seaside dunes and then on the first sandy shelf risen behind them lies the links. At first sight it is almost pastoral, being enclosed within stone walls on the three landward sides and from the sea-dunes by a long thick plantation of buckthorn. From the club house you see the sea, down and beyond and away—you hardly hear it at all: at once a noble vista and of great elegance. 'Elegance' is, I think, the word. Muirfield is neat, perfectly tailored, it has the reserve, yet the ease, of its aristocratic tradition. Every shot must here be placed correctly and precisely; that is true of any good links, but at Muirfield the danger is in its seeming openness. It doesn't *look* as if you'll be in great trouble if you are crooked. Never was a links so beautifully, unobtrusively, devilishly bunkered: there are about 170 bunkers. And the bunkers themselves all have neat, upright, symmetrically layered faces, built of turves and utterly unyielding: if you lie close under them, it is best to play out sideways; the sand is always raked so that it seems almost a breach of etiquette to disturb the ribbed surface, but you may disturb it, deeply and several times before escaping. Bunkers lurk everywhere for the least weakness, fade, or draw, lipping into the greens, swallowing your ball like medicine—without pleasure but with an air of moral eagerness—as if to say "this will do him good"—genuinely meaning so, and without the least rancour. But Muirfield *wants* you to play well. There is this subtle difference between the attitudes of links. Like schoolmasters, some are out to get just mechanical repetition (without sense, if need be); some are out to trap you, to make you answer wrongly even if you *know* the right answer; very few are really eager to get their pupils on, to develop them and stimulate them imaginatively, while keeping the strictest rein on accuracy and discipline. Muirfield is among these few best of teachers; for it is essentially lovable, yet to be respected and never to be 'ragged'.

Walter Hagen, that great and jovial golfer, dared to take liberties with the 8th, playing his drive away to the right and approaching the green from the wrong angle, short-cutting, and cutting the bunkers. The hole was, no, not offended exactly, but quizzical and critical of such behaviour and quietly requested the committee to act. So buckthorn-trees were planted, in case Hagen returned, or the contagion spread. I do not suppose a word was spoken. Muirfield is "sea-green incorruptible".

8th hole, Muirfield.
(455 YARDS)

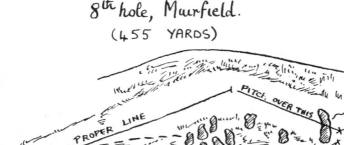

The lay-out of the links is essentially in key with its general tone. The club house stands at the centre of the south side of the rectangle of land and the first nine holes go clockwise right round the perimeter, enclosing the second nine within them. Thus, looking from the smoking-room window the first tee is away to the left, the ninth green and tenth tee to the right, and the eighteenth green immediately in front.

Whatever the wind's quarter you will have it from all angles before you have finished.

Muirfield, as you would expect, is most exquisitely well kept. It has decided against such things as 'bogeys' and 'standard scratch scores'—it just ignores them. Likewise it has no special 'championship' tees—holding, with reason, that the back tees, the medal tees, of a links are the true test of its golf, and that super-tiger tees throw out the bunkering and general flow of the design. Decorums are not to be outraged. There is a refreshing air of formal informality about this club, which is unique in golf.

I have not attempted to describe the links hole by hole; for it is of a very close texture, so to speak, the holes lead one from another as in a fugue. The beauty of the 3rd lies in its relation to the 8th, etc. Indeed one is continually thinking of it in terms of the eighteenth century: and what is best of that atmosphere seems to have been miraculously preserved alive: players still

> *"ply*
> *Their pond'rous weapons, and the greens defy."*

It is a pity there is no poet now to chronicle them!

Muirfield lies just to the east of Gullane (southerners, note: pronounced Gill'n), where a really astonishing amount of golf goes on. If you approach Gullane from Edinburgh, rounding a bend in Aberlady, you come to a flat expanse of foreshore, and across the other side of it rises a long swell of heathy bluff, a great whale's back of above-sea country; a vast area of Golf. Gullane has three courses, and some argue that Gullane No. 1 is superior to Muirfield; but it will always be the second-string, qualifying-round course, while Muirfield remains the Championship test— and this is just about as it should be. At any rate, anyone visiting the district can be sure of a game!

MUIRFIELD

Hole	Length		Hole	Length
1	453		10	480
2	353		11	359
3	382		12	380
4	192		13	153
5	510		14	458
6	458		15	393
7	157		16	193
8	455		17	513
9	490		18	427
Out	3450		In	3356
			Out	3450
			Total	6806

Note.—There is no Standard Scratch Score for this course.

LOCAL RULES

1. The boundaries of the course are the walls and fences surrounding it. A ball played outside these is 'out of bounds'.

Note.—A ball played into Archerfield Wood, and into any field under cultivation, is irrecoverable.

2. A ball lying in a rabbit scrape or rabbit hole through the green may be lifted and dropped within a club's length, keeping the point where the ball lay in the rabbit scrape or rabbit hole directly between the ball and the hole, under penalty of one stroke. If the rabbit scrape or rabbit hole be in a hazard, the ball may be lifted and dropped under penalty of one stroke in the hazard within a club's length of the spot from which it was lifted.

3. A ball lying in a rabbit scrape or rabbit hole on the putting green may be lifted and placed outside the rabbit scrape or rabbit hole as near as possible to the spot from which it was lifted, but not nearer to the hole under penalty of one stroke.

4. A ball lying on any surface specially prepared for putting, other than that of the hole being played, shall be lifted and dropped on the course without penalty, as near as possible to the place where it lay, but not nearer the hole being approached.

NORTH BERWICK

NORTH BERWICK has an east and a west end. "Me and the mate likes ends," said the Captain, cutting the pudden' in half. I like North Berwick like that.

The east end has cliffs and a lien on the Bass Rock; the west end has a wonderful stretch of sandy-rocky bays, and sand-dunes, towards the point off which Fidra Island lies.

There are two golf courses: the east-end one, the Burgh or Municipal course, climbs the cliff and ambles along its top; and *it allows Sunday play*:—it is no offence to it to say that that is a recommendation. The golf is pleasant and it is difficult, or should be, to lose your ball: there is plenty of fairway and plenty of room to wander. The views from the course are superb. But it is not really upon the Burgh course that the fame of North Berwick rests. It is upon its west-end course, the West Links, which runs along the lovely shore westward from the town.

Let me explain here, to the visitor accustomed to southern English golf, that club houses on many Scottish courses belong exclusively to *clubs*—who have playing rights over a publicly owned course. They are *not* the place to pay your green fee, change, drink, or eat.

For example: North Berwick. You must go to the starter's box; book your starting time from him, if need be; pay your green fee; get your ticket (and keep it, you may be asked for it) and start. Golf is, so very much more, a part of Scottish life. You walk changed and ready and carrying your clubs, from your home to the tee, play the round, and walk home again. If you want a drink afterwards, well, you take your clubs into the pub with you: but primarily golf is a *game* simply to be played for itself, and not for its stimulatory adjuncts. You would think from this that the Scots were all very good at golf, but they are not! I find it a curious thing, with all the facilities for cheap golf that still exist in Scotland, that Scots do not dominate the professional and amateur game: it is far, far too long since the Open was won by a

Scot (or the Amateur, for that matter). These reflections are prompted particularly by a visit to North Berwick.

There, on the little tiddly toddlers' course, opposite the Marine Hotel, children are swinging it from the age of three or so—lots of them, and not all English visitors, unless English children are all brilliant mimics of a Scottish accent. Indeed, wherever you go in Scotland you see children with clubs: what happens to them all? Is it entirely economic, or is there something a little too loose in the full Scottish swing?

There are the little children. Now let us walk to the first tee at North Berwick proper. I have sat there three full days:

> *On the first day I saw*
> *Swings without law;*
> *On the second,*
> *I saw swings unreckoned;*
> *On the third,*
> *Swings fantastically absurd. . . .*

They were Scottish swings; they were of all ages and sexes. Now, do all the worst golfers in Scotland go holidaying at North Berwick? I remember in Robert K. Risk's "Songs of the Links" a parody of Rudyard Kipling which went, I think,

> *There are fourscore ways and three*
> *Of hitting from the tee,*
> *And every single one of them is right.*

Let the perfectionist stand at cover-point from No. 1 (or should I say 'Garry-point' for the hole is called 'Point Garry'?), and he will have far too many sitters to hold. North Berwick is, really, a very good course indeed; one has only to look at the 78's and 82's which win its serious competitions, but it must meanwhile suffer, like zoo elephants, every conceivable kind of duffer on its back uncomplainingly.

Are the fairways too wide? Aberration would cross their frontiers. What North Berwick has done for its golf is something like *The Reader's Digest* or a "People's *Hamlet*". Here is a précis of golf, a simplified plot. It is sheerly idiotic to try to guard against every kind of golfing lunacy—only to ensure that most kinds cannot complain of the inadequate padding of their cells. North Berwick is charmingly padded.

The very first hole sets the tone. It is a mad hole, anyway. Across its expanse pass, in endless rout, the holiday columns attacking the sea: backwards and forwards they go, the warp of this tapestry of which golfing rabbits are the woof. You must push off with some iron along a fairway thick with traffic and stop short of a bunkered hill whence you flick up on to a sideways-tilting green which is prepared to decant you back on to the beach. Par and bogey are 4; my Gallup Poll over three August days averaged 7-plus.

If you are a modest or retiring golfer the first three holes, in the season, will profit the psychiatrists no end. No shot that is not observed, and mocked, by young men and maidens, old men and children—and in particular your tee shot to No. 2, called 'The Sea'. From an elevated 'pulpit' tee you can cut your golfing sermon by driving briefly on to the beach, or steer slowly round, or bore well and Calvinistically inland, or flog across with a secret draw, like an Archdeacon trying on a Bishop's topper; and so on to the green with a longish second. Now, at No. 3—('Trap', it is called)—comes the first jump over a strong stone wall, and over it your second to the hole must go. Town-side is public; west of it is yours for your green fee. And once on the fourth tee you have the promised land ahead. The 4th-15th are really pleasant, sane, golf—at any price.

By now, you have ceased to be so harried by dogs and their owners, and owners and their dogs, and you find yourself hitting into a bottle-neck with all mystery beyond. The 4th is a longish one-shot hole into a defile with rocks poking from the soil, on the left, to entice a death or glory ricochet. On the fifth tee a real, wide-open-space of golfing country opens before you in a great open right-angled triangle. The right angle is made by the fifth hole to the eighth hole along the landward side, and the ninth pointing straight seaward to the dunes. On the fifth tee you get one of the loveliest views in golf, seeing the bay and the gold of dunes along to the right of you and a whole tract of golf within them, green and beflagged. Away, right, is the Firth with its islands, Lamb Island in particular, and the herring-gulls, eternally hungry,

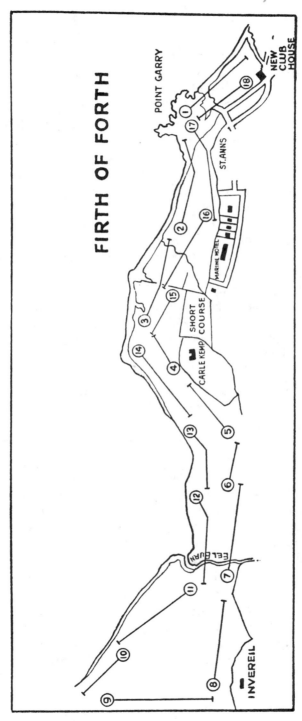

NORTH BERWICK—Plan of the course

kerlowking-kerlowking from them, which, if this were a desert, would drive one crazy very soon. But as it is, holes of stirring golf stretch ahead west, towards the woods where Dirleton goes down to the sea, and Muirfield hides discreetly beyond. All these holes, 4th–15th, are, or could be, good golf holes. They are easy; easy to do in one over bogey. But to score them properly the shots need playing, and placing, and playing. At the 7th—the Eil, or Eel, Burn gets into the way of all but eels. The views at this point of the links are quite ravishing particularly from the fairways, and what else is there? Do not let us pretend that North Berwick is a championship course: not at least a major one, for the Scottish Boys have fought it out here—world-beaters of the future?

To return to our theme, is it possible to guess from North Berwick why Scots are not the world's greatest golfers? (I know that North Berwick is a holiday resort and that it caters for the holiday-swatter, but still . . .) With all humility I do suggest that the Scots have taken the rough with the smooth far too literally; bunkers are the statutory form of punishment, but one gets away with the indifferent stroke far too easily. As I say, I know that North Berwick is a special case, for it is so be-golfed that hold-ups for ball-hunting would throw it into chaos . . . but even Muirfield is, to my mind, too gentle. Compare that beautiful heather course at Blairgowrie (which everyone should play on) with Walton Heath! Is Walton Heath too narrow?

But, maybe, in the end, it *is* a question of economics and the best Scots golfers are not able to compete in tournament golf. Nevertheless, it worries me; and if living on the coast of Sussex it worries *me*, it must surely drive the patriotic Scot to frenzy.

To return to North Berwick! The 10th–15th are all good golf. If the wind prevails westerly you will have it behind you. The 13th is a unique hole. A drive and a pitch; but the pitch is over a stone wall into a bowl green set narrow-ways against you and just the other side. To pitch exactly on the wall has been known; to rush at and refuse the fence repeatedly, like the favourite at a point-to-point, is not unknown either. Anyway, head well down and pitch well up is the recipe.

'Perfection' is the name of the next hole. I must admit that it is not at all my idea of perfection, though it has other sterling, or

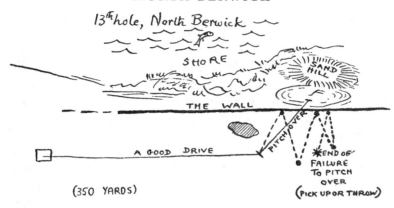

13ᵗʰhole, North Berwick

SHORE

SAND HILL

THE WALL

A GOOD DRIVE

PITCH OVER

★END OF FAILURE TO PITCH OVER (PICK UP OR THROW)

(350 YARDS)

should one now say, dollar qualities; as has the 'Redan' which is reproduced on the National Links of America. 'Perfection' has drama. A good drive, and you will be faced with a steep blind slope—to pitch over, as it seems, bang into the sea. A high target-post at the back of the hidden green stands on the very edge of the rocks. There is plenty of room over the hill—twenty yards or so, before the green, and a pitch a bit to the left will come in nicely across the slope with more margin of error possible than the dead bull's-eye shot. Perhaps there always ought to be a bit of luck as an element in perfection, as beauty is enhanced by mystery and irregularity. 'The Redan', the short 15th, comes next. I'm sorry, but I can't see it as a great short hole; and I beg leave to wonder what other short holes the American architect had seen and rejected in its favour. But it looks nice and it looks, too, rather 'artificial', which may have been the source of its charm; for American golf architects love 'folding' and 'moulding' and would, I believe, *really* like to work in some substance like plastic, and pour a whole links out in great prefabricated slabs. So, I feel that huge concrete casts of the 'Redan' may very well be used all over the States and covered with earth, sand, turf, and so on. . . . But to the next tee: back over the wall we go into the hurly-burly, skirting the children's course, where

> *Such, such were the joys*
> *When we all, girls & boys,*
> *In our youth time were seen*
> *On the Echoing Green.*

95

and admiring the Scottish-baronial pile of the Marine Hotel.

No. 17 takes you back up to Point Garry and is a good hole, like 'Perfection', save that the pitch is only semi-blind; and from the last tee a cut drive could earn immortality by denting a Rolls-Royce. All along the right is the road where you park your car; but there is a world of room to the left and the chance of denting any number of holiday-makers, or even players who have only hit one blow.

Before leaving the links let us recall a famous remark from the early 1830's: "He takes more time to tee his ball than any three men, pulls up as much grass as would summer a hunter, and after all he ends in an abortive puff." The number of abortive puffs upon the links of North Berwick if laid end to end would stretch from —— to ——. (You can fill in the divots as you please.)

Before leaving North Berwick you ought to look in at Ben Sayers' shop where, surely, one of the most varied ranges of clubs in the world is made—starting from a tiny wooden club for two-and-a-half-year-olds! It is fascinating to watch golf clubs being made. The persimmon of wooden-club heads comes only from America, in blocks. These must be kept at an even temperature —and wooden clubs for export to hot climates are specially 'dried out' before finishing, lest the wood swell or shrink, and the metal soles and inlaid faces buckle or warp! Your irons begin as long rustless iron bars which are heated in the forge, worked by the smith under a mechanical stamp or hammer (I don't know its technical name) first for the hose, then for the head, and they pass through at least half a dozen different processes, including sand-blasting the faces to dull the finish, and every club is weighed to a fraction of an ounce. I had no idea, not having seen clubmaking since I was a boy, what modern hand-made clubmaking entailed. I am glad I know, for now I can never, never blame my clubs again.

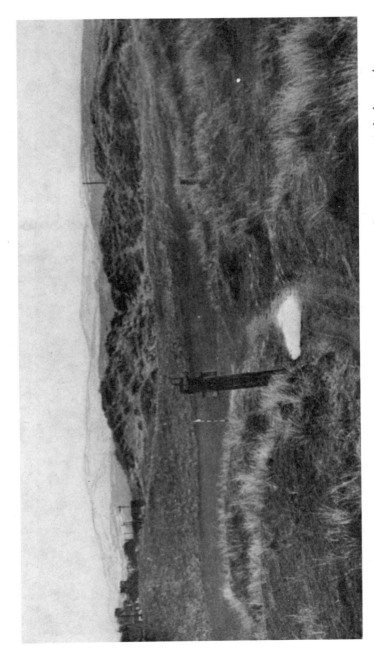

ABERDOVEY: 3rd Green, from path to 4th tee. The Cader bunker and periscope on tee in background.

CARNOUSTIE : Approaching 5th Green. 6th hole behind with practice field beyond.

GANTON : The 11th, from the tee.

GLENEAGLES : View of 14th fairway, King's Course.

HOYLAKE : The 13th—'The Rushes'.

HUNSTANTON : 1st Green, with 2nd tee in the foreground.

LITTLE ASTON: The 17th Green as seen from the approach shot.

MOORTOWN : The short 8th.

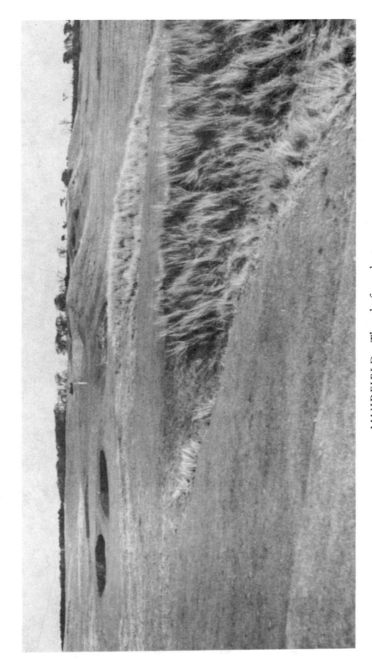

MUIRFIELD : The 4th, from the tee.

NORTH BERWICK: 14th Green, from top-left of ridge over which blind second must be played.

PORTRUSH: 5th hole. Players walking in line of drive. Green to right by fence on sea-edge.

ST. ANDREWS: The Road hole, seen at right angles to the line of play. 18th Green and Clubhouse in background.

SUNNINGDALE : The 10th, from the tee.

WALTON HEATH: The short 17th, from behind the tee.

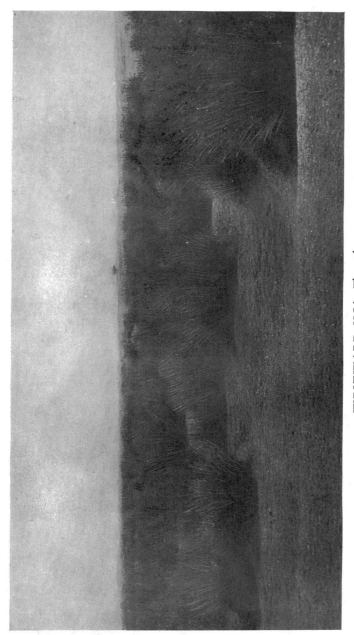

WESTWARD HO!: The rushes.

WORLINGTON: The second shot to the 6th.

SCORE CARD

Hole	Name	Length	S.S.S.	Hole	Name	Length	S.S.S.
1	Point Garry (Out)	330	4	10	Eastward Ho!	157	3
				11	Bo's'n's Locker	520	5
2	Sea	432	4	12	Bass	360	4
3	Trap	463	5	13	Pit	350	4
4	Carl Kemp	200	3	14	Perfection	382	4
5	Bunker's Hill	378	4	15	Redan	195	3
6	Quarry	152	3	16	Gate	400	5
7	Eil Burn	360	4	17	Point Garry (In)	470	5
8	Linkhouse	439	5				
9	Mizzen Top	508	5	18	Home	275	4
	Out	3262	37		In	3109	37
					Out	3262	37
					Total	6371	74

LOCAL RULES
(For Medal and Match Play)

1. The ditch opposite the Marine Hotel and the Eil Burn are recognised water hazards; a ball lying within the slopes of either may be treated as in the hazard.

All walls on the course and the beach are recognised hazards.

2. Should a ball be played into the sea, it shall, if recoverable, be dropped on the beach within two clubs' length of the water under penalty of one stroke. If the ball cannot be recovered or dropped on the beach it shall be treated as lost.

3. Should a ball lie on the road crossing the second fairway, it may be lifted and dropped behind the road under penalty of one stroke.

4. Should a ball be played on to the short course, or into Carl Kemp grounds, or over any lines, fences, or walls bounding the course (except the wall at the 13th hole and the wall on the north of the 3rd hole), or on to the metalled road bounding the 18th hole, or on to the gravelled enclosure round the club house, it shall be considered out of bounds.

Note.—The short course east of the first wall is bounded by lines drawn from a white painted post in the Marine ditch to marks painted on the above wall and the south boundary wall. The posts along the road at the 18th hole are immovable obstructions, and shall be treated as such. The penalty for out of bounds is loss of distance only.

5. Should a ball be played on to the club maker's shop or the caddies' shelter, or within the surrounding sleeper fence, it shall be considered out of bounds.

6. Should a ball be played on to any putting ground other than that to which the player is playing, it shall be lifted and dropped clear of the green, but not nearer the hole.

Note.—When two holes are on contiguous greens, such greens shall be considered as one.

7. If a ball lie in a rabbit scrape, it may be lifted and dropped behind the scrape under penalty of one stroke. If the scrape be in a bunker or hazard, the ball must be dropped in the bunker or hazard.

PORTRUSH
Royal Portrush

—————————◇—————————

PORTRUSH is H. S. Colt's masterpiece (though he may not agree with me). Certainly the ground is worthy of a great links; there is spaciousness and grandeur; these ranges of sandhills are, to ordinary sandhills, what the Alps are to the Grampians. Out to sea lie the rocky ridges of the Skerries—originally, I imagine, the coastline, for either side of the links the cliffs soon rise again dour and grey: but within the Skerries the Atlantic has swelled and broken, and piled in rollers of sand, creating a stretch of country on the grand scale. The sandhills rise shelf upon shelf, and it is upon the most landward shelf that the links is set. One has the curious feeling of playing along a cliff top—high above the sea, but the whole *cliff* is made of sandhills. I have never seen a links which so invites adjectives of nobility and size; of space and height. Sometimes in dreams one has the sensation of flying or gliding gently and easily as a gull from the cliff-side. Portrush is flying golf—one longs to take off after the ball, and indeed the air from the Atlantic is so fresh that such levitation does not seem impossible.

The rough is composed of wild briar rose, thick, long claggy grasses and (if there is a wet season) moss; the whole compound has the consistency of porridge and is entirely hellish; a kind of Sargasso. I speak first of the rough because Portrush is proud—and rightly proud—of the fact that it has very few bunkers. (You may remember that another giant, Carnoustie, is busy removing its surplus.)

You will not be impressed by the first hole, though you may be irritated. How wide the fairway, which slopes gently down and away with a rather meadowy inland look; how well to the left that boundary fence; how far to the right that other fence; yet in the days of stroke and distance a scratch player has been known to play 13 from the tee—that means six consecutive shots out of bounds!

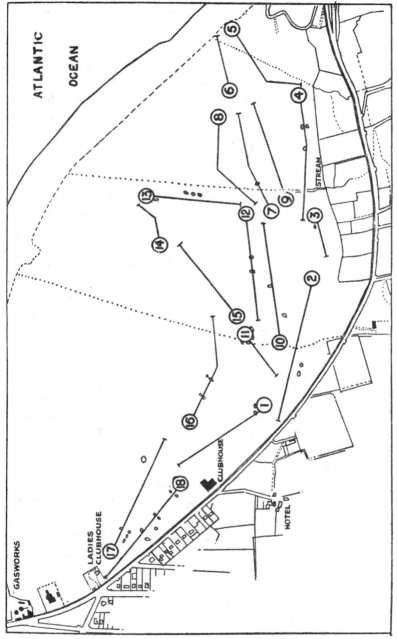

PORTRUSH—Plan of the course

It is so *unlike* the first drive at Hoylake, so charmingly obvious and avoidable, and yet . . . A straight long drive and all is well. I think Portrush *is* particularly a driver's links. There is trouble in front of most tees, real ghastly give-it-up-at-once kind of trouble; but the carries—even from the back tees—are not fierce. Anything crooked goes into the porridge—there's no chance of landing on another fairway and getting away with a long, wild wicked one. No, the ball from the tee must be hit straight and true. That, I know, is one of the oldest clichés of the game; at Portrush you'd better forget it's a cliché and come freshly upon it as a great Discovery: the one magical secret of golf! Note that I have just put the adjectives 'straight' and 'long' in that order. Second shots are a joy, there are plenty of opportunities to use wood; and where that is so, you are given that special kind of do-or-dare shot which *may* reach the green—yet, if hit correctly, gives you entire pleasure even if you do not. Such a heavenly swoop is the second shot at No. 2. Away goes the ball downhill (so to speak) through a curving pass, or defile, just out of sight, to reappear at rest across a further gully and on the edge of the green. There are lots of chances for the pitch-and-run from twenty yards—owing to this lack of bunkers—for Colt has placed his greens brilliantly, achieving here, I think, the perfect mating of the old-fashioned cup-in-a-hollow and the new-fashioned mushroom-on-a-hill style of green. Owing to the largesse of Nature he has been able to place his greens *up* and still to have them among hills whose shoulders and slopes diminish their size to pinheads. This makes the long second, or the short third, always an exciting and exhilarating shot.

From the second green you climb steeply up to the third tee and from it you have one of the most marvellous views: landscape and seascape and golfscape. There is something quite ravishing to the golfer in these winding viridian ways towards the emeralds with the bright flags stiff in the wind; the 'silence and slow time' of it and the pacing, intent figures. And on the third tee, here, the tract of sandhills appears so vast, the human figures so small that one looks with a hawk's or an airman's eye, and having spent this lyrical moment, like stout Cortez and all his men, the wonder gives place to the wild surmise: how long this shaft is! how small this club-head, how minute this ball! How far the green! *How can I do this at all?* Luckily for you the 3rd is a short hole, and not a very difficult one. It is called 'Islay' and there *is* Islay out on the horizon. But on, to the fourth hole—a beautiful two-and-a-half shotter like the word 'every', which you can give three or two syllables to, as you choose. There is an out-of-bounds fence along the right and a well-placed fairway bunker nudging you over towards it, and another of those long hopeful seconds taking you to the mouth of a green beautifully placed in among dunes.

The greens are, on the whole, easy to putt on. They are not over-large and not too full of borrows. One should never get the horrors on them. They are greens for the attacking putter.

Now for the 5th: one of the most romantic holes in the world. (And this is a great romantic links.) Standing on the highest point of the dunes inland (and we have come east all along the inside perimeter between dunes and wild hill-side), you turn at right angles and face directly seaward. The ground collapses down towards the sea in a huge series of lumpy mounds, a steeply sloping field of giant molehills; the gradient is violent and away below and to the right, on the edge above the sea, is the green. It looks miles away. But as the ball flies it is only a drive and a No. 3 or 4. This drive is really enchanting. You must hit well to the left of where you'd like to—for over the hills and less far away, there is a fairway which you can't quite see from the tee. The more you bite off on the direct line the more likely you are to land among the briary hills and to take 3 more (the 1st backwards and the 3rd sideways) to reach the fairway. I cannot begin to describe the fantasy of this awesome and beautiful golf hole. It is like playing down a long doglegged waterfall with the green a still, deep, green pool below the rapids. And if you go over *that*, you go down, down, into the sea. It is well that one turns inland to the next hole and that it is a long one-shot hole of a reasonably tame nature: but only one generation from wildness, like a tiger-cub born in a zoo. The talons on its green paws know what to do.

Since 1945 two new holes have been made in these first nine— and very good ones they are—in particular the two-shot 8th, a sharp dogleg to the right whose angle is perfect, as the straight, long, driver will find. The green is a not very long but very narrow strip between sandhills and if you are not opposite the entrance your second will sink into the sticky and prickly obscurity which surrounds the green.

Like the old song "Yes, we have no bananas" it is "Yes, we have no sand-bunkers" . . . you may remember how the song went on to catalogue what other fruit and vegetables were in stock. The 8th will tell you what *it* has in stock, if you go crooked. There is a refreshment hut at the turn; and the 10th is not too cruel, after it, being a nice steady-going chap of a bogey-five character, and the 11th is a charmingly precipitous short hole called 'The Feather Bed'. You just flick the ball away straight and down it drops plumb—into one of the bunkers which draw a cordon round the green, as if it were wanted for some crime and was about to make a bolt for it. The 12th has a very small seductive tortoiseshell of a green from which second shots retreat rejected in a thwarted way. I must admit that I do not admire this hole as much as I am told I should. I feel it has somehow had its sting removed, it feels bowdlerised. But for the next two holes my admiration is unbounded. The 13th, like the 5th, points seaward, but this time you drive up a steady slope to the crest of a ridge. Across a small valley lies the green, again on the sea-edge with a deep rushy chasm to its left and a steep convex slope to its right—in fact it is placed exactly on the top of a large dune, and it needs a nice straight, high No. 5 into the wind or through it. This is a beautifully proportioned hole and gives no hint of what is to come.

Stepping off the green westwards, a marvellous view presents itself: you are on the end of a striding-edge with an almost sheer drop to the right. Down below is a great hidden valley containing *another whole golf links*! You can have no real conception of this small grandeur till you see it. I must emphasise again the *scale* of these ranges of dunes at Portrush—they are Alpine, Apennine, *foreign*. On this fourteenth tee you are standing upon the point of a V, the right-hand arm goes out guarding the coast; in the middle is the valley, and along the left-hand arm, exactly along its *edge*, is this next hole called with tactful understatement 'Calamity Corner'. It is two hundred yards long and there is no room on the left, which is the wild rushy crest of the ridge. A yard to the right

14ᵗʰ hole, Portrush,
Calamity Corner.
(206 YARDS)

and over you go, sheer down this grass cliff whose gradient must be 1 in 1. It is a romantic chasm, an opening of hell, and to escape from it it is necessary to defy gravity, taking your stance almost like a fly on a wall, and striking a rocket-shot up to the zenith of heaven. You can do this any number of times, for I almost dare not say that the lies on this cold hill's side are not, well, exactly favourable to pyrotechnics. Having encompassed this, we play 'Purgatory' which swoops all the way down the landward side of the ridge in a superb toboggan-run to a green at the bottom— another less-feathery bed. The drive at Purgatory is very thrilling, for the tee is just below the horizon-line and you hit madly into thin air—the ball disappears away down almost like dropping a penny into a well. These three holes 13–14–15 should be done in 4, 3, 4!

The 16th is a very fine long two-shot hole, notable for its tee, which is sixty-five yards long. If one is at the back end, it is rather like the runway of an aircraft-carrier. The hole doglegs to the right and your second must carry some diagonal traps before reaching safety. There's a grass gully to the left of the green, and a bank on the right.

The finish is a little disappointing after the adventures and explorations we have had. True, the drive at the 17th ought to disappear over the end of a long hog's-back or steer exactly between it and a great rearing sandhill whose near face is all bunker;

but once through this Scylla and Charybdis you come out on to the flat, on to almost a field, an inland-looking stretch of harmless grass-and-bunkers. These last two holes are both long, and two steady 5's are not beyond the bounds of probability. But left with two 5's to *win*, I can see them dwindling into 6's without one's quite knowing how or why. If Portrush can be said to have any bad holes, I must record that I think the 18th is at any rate not a good hole! It is, so to speak, comforting, but *officially* comforting and without affection, like an income-tax rebate or the kiss of a strange aunt.

The Championship Committee was right as can be to choose this links for the first Open Championship to be held beyond the sea.

PORTRUSH

Hole	Name	Yards	S.S.S.	Hole	Name	Yards	S.S.S.
1	Hughie's	400	4	10	Dhu Varren	473	5
2	Giant's Grave	510	5	11	Feather Bed	167	3
3	Islay	160	3	12	Causeway	400	4
4	Primrose Dell	455	4	13	Skerries	380	4
5	White Rocks	398	4	14	Calamity		
6	Harry Colt's	200	3		Corner	206	3
7	Tavern	426	4	15	Purgatory	367	4
8	Himalayas	380	4	16	Stables	440	4
9	Warren	444	5	17	Glenarm	520	5
				18	Greenaway	476	5
	Out	3373	36				

In	3429	37
Out	3373	36
Total	6802	73

LOCAL RULES

1. A ball lying in any of the burns on the course, either in water or between the banks, may be lifted and dropped behind under the penalty of one stroke.

2. A ball lying on a green other than the one played at shall be lifted and dropped off the green without penalty, at a not less distance from the hole played at.

3. A ball lying in a rabbit scrape may be lifted and dropped behind without penalty provided that the ball cannot be touched by a club placed across the hole or scrape in any direction.

4. A ball lying within one club's length of the paling at the 1st, 2nd, 4th, 11th, and 16th holes may be lifted and dropped within two clubs' length of the paling not nearer the hole, under the penalty of one stroke.

5. A ball lying on any road, or outside any paling or in the club house grounds, or outside the boundary of the course, shall be 'out of bounds'. A ball lying on any path on the course shall be played from where it lies.

6. A ball played on to the strand beyond the 5th green is out of bounds if lying on the sea side of the two white posts.

RYE

Like every seaside links, Rye has been through many metamorphoses. Its present shape is post-1945, and is likely to be at least semi-final. There are still eighteen holes, and there is no more land left. Each incarnation has been a contraction. Once there were holes to landward of the road, once there were holes beyond the coastguards' cottages. There are five short holes now. Do not imagine from this that Rye is child's play. You may not need your brassie, but you will need extra skill with the irons. There is a kind of small fierceness about Rye, as if one were looking at a wild cat through a magnifying-glass and imagining a tiger. Many of us golfers, may I say, regard our own images in just this way; and Rye has a taming way with it; tigers on the first tee may be reduced to domestic tabbies mewing over spilt milk by the turn.

If you suffer from lack of balance, this is not the course for you: it is seldom that you get a flat stance, and this is one of Rye's real tests. The fairways nearly all undulate and you will find you must play a full shot from the side of a miniature down and one foot on a level with your nose. Going from Rye to a flatter terrain, you feel like coming ashore after a voyage—the pavement still seems to heave under your feet—yes, you need sea-legs here.

Rye is the good iron-player's paradise; and four of its five short holes are great holes—as a 'clutch' of short holes I would back them against any course in the world. The fifth of the short holes (the 17th) is a controversial hole—it has bitter enemies. It is just over two hundred yards long, flat, and the green slides quite steeply from right to left and there are bunkers on the left. The purists complain that a straightly struck spoon shot will pitch on the slope of the green and kick left into trouble. Along the right, from tee to green, runs a gravelly track; and a shot just too much to the right will pitch in it, and like as not go hopping along in it like a rabbit or leap out to the right—never, it seems, never to the left on to the green. (P. H. F. White did the hole in 1 to beat L. G. Crawley, once, in a match during the President's Putter.)

I've got that hole over first because I think every other hole on the course to be first-class, some, as they say, more than others.

But before going out to play let us contemplate the club house, which is a real gem of the great corrugated-iron period of club-house architecture. It has recently been restored and roughcast and the interior has lost, alas, its original racy pitch-pine smell— but it is still the right rambling shape and you can still walk straight into dark cupboards full of bound volumes of *Punch* when attempting to escape. It is also difficult to find the way in. Once inside all is hospitable, warm, and friendly. Visitors are bound sooner or later to discover the President's Putter in its glass case, like the branch of some exotic vine hung with its cluster of great white grapes. Certainly the vintages of the last thirty years of amateur golf may be learnt there: *Château Holderness* and *Château Wethered* are the principal, but the *Tolley* year was good, beautifully smooth on the palate, also the *Crawley* and more recently —a sparkling wine this—the *Lucas de la Main Gauche*.

But, sir, who *is* the President and what is his Putter? The President is the president of the Oxford and Cambridge Golfing Society and his putter—once the property of Hugh Kirkaldy— has been played for annually, in the dark days of January, by its members, since 1920, when J. L. Low, who was then President, instituted the competition.

The association of the Society with Rye is a long and happy one, dating back to a time that Mr. Darwin—long may he be President of the Society!—does not "precisely remember". The links was laid out in the mid-'nineties—1894—and the Society was formed in 1898. Sometime, then, in the early years of the century, the golf club invited the Society to regard Rye as its home green. I dare say that Parson Tindall had a certain amount to do with this invitation. He was a fine athlete, and down from Cambridge he started a prep. school near Hastings and together with another sporting reverend gentleman, a doctor, and H. S. Colt founded the club. As at most seaside links there is one major range of sandhills —the first line from the sea—and a secondary spur inland from it. Luckily, at Rye, there is some room on the seaward side of the main spur and the links works its way on both sides, or over at an angle, and in one case along the top of the dunes. This hole—the new 4th—is surely one of the greatest two-shot holes in golf? The fairway is narrow anyway, and narrows the farther you drive. Since it is high up, sliced off the top of the dune, there is a steep descent on either side. To the left is a large and deep grass and sand crater, to the right, the whole length of the hole, a thick slope at a steep angle down. A drive cut wildly enough will curve across fairway, above bank and rough, and land far away down on the third fairway, leaving a full shot to be lifted long and diagonally up over the dune-side back to the higher level. But suppose your drive is straight and lies on the narrow plateau, the second shot is one of great difficulty and skill. The fairway slopes down to a bottle-neck, through which it tilts and continues not flat, but with a considerable bias to the left, so that any second shot which is straight but short will fall away left and leave a cunning uphill chip or run-up to the green. That is, however, safe. The right-hand edge all along, and including the green itself, falls as steeply away to the right as ever and a cut second will go down, down, down among the dead men, leaving a high blind pitch. The green itself is set at a perfectly fiendish tilt; going uphill from the front to the back and sideways from the right to the left.

The perfect second, I suppose, is played with a trace of fade to pitch on the bottom left-hand corner of the green and run a little inwards and upwards towards the centre. The prevailing wind, which is on the left shoulder, will accentuate the slightest inaccuracy in this shot and whirl you over the edge. A 5 will win this hole as often as not. It is a magnificent golf hole, and no words of mine can more than hint at its splendours and despairs.

Rye is full of such ups and downs of emotion. There are many dark declivities, side slopes, and Anglo-Saxon attitudes. The thirteenth hole—the sea hole—has a blind second, right over the hills, with acres of purgatorial penance for a hook. It's old-fashioned, I know, but the moment at the top, when you see a ball safe on the green—or your stomach begins to curdle with unripe forebodings and premonitions of sandy excavations—is one I would not lose.

Another lovely hole is the 15th, played from the ridge to a very

4th hole, Rye

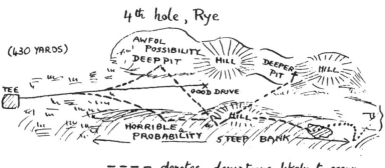

(430 YARDS)

AWFUL POSSIBILITY
DEEP PIT
HILL
DEEPER PIT
HILL
TEE
GOOD DRIVE
HILL
HORRIBLE PROBABILITY
STEEP BANK

– – – – denotes deviations likely to occur.

undulant fairway. A shoulder of dune juts from the left and all
along the right is a sandy valley whence progress is possible in
short flops towards the hole. From mid-fairway you can see only
the top of the pin, and between you and it the fairway narrows
to the point of a V and turns into a small hogbacked spur beyond
which lies the green—farther beyond than it looks. Apart from
the 17th there is not a dull hole at Rye, for the whole links is in
larger or smaller green waves of ground, so sealike one almost
expects them suddenly to rear up and break.

Rye is a great iron-player's course, and it is no wonder that
L. G. Crawley is its local maestro. For the timid player from the
tee it is really formidable, and there is not a single hole where a
topped drive will rabbit its way to the fairway. The carries are
not huge but they are always there, and there is not a great deal
of room to stray.

In the dead of winter when we play for the Putter—let me
confess to being a resident and member of Rye as well as of the
Society—this links is as difficult as anywhere in the world. The
sou'wester sweeps in from the sea and is nowhere a help, nowhere at all, and the greens, even in January, are keen and slippery
as eels.

Were there enough hotel accommodation I can see no reason
why Rye should not be the venue for at least a minor championship. As it is, the University golf match constantly returns to it in
March, a month I recommend to any visitor—for, let us admit,
Rye is not at its best in summer, it is so *very* seaside, the lies get so
light they burst in spurts of sand, and the whole surface becomes

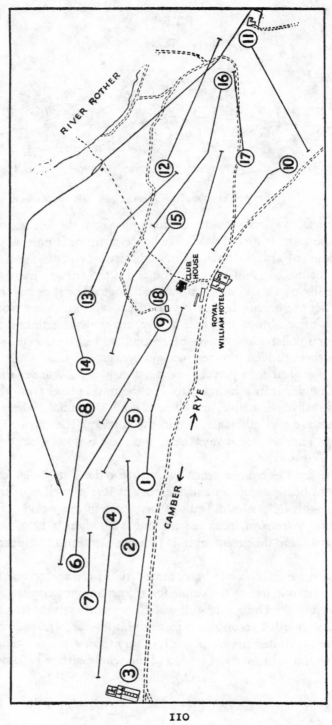

RYE—Plan of the course

too loosely knit for comfort. It's very good for the golf, if not for the temperament. As an Autumn to Spring course it is ideal, and you are dryshod anywhen. But, of course, it is the Putter weekend which makes Rye unique. The motto upon the medal, "Primus inter pares", has been translated by A. C. M. Croome as "He was lucky to win", and that is true. For Rye is dreadfully hard on an eighteen-hole match. A good start is everything—there is nowhere you can recover—the pace—the rhythm of the round—is that of the quarter-mile, flat out all the way. (Parson Tyndall held the record for the quarter-mile for many years, oddly enough.)

Assuming you start from the first tee you are immediately in the toils, for No. 2 is a brilliantly cunning short hole, and more 4's than 3's are likely there any day. The secret of short-hole play I believe is very simple. *Always be past the pin*. Nearly all the trouble is only as far as pin-high. Certainly this is true at Rye. A straight shot just over the back is far safer than the perfect length *just* out of direction. At the new seventh hole right among the dunes nowhere is safe (except on) but through. The same is true of the 14th and 17th. In each case you are left with a straight-forward chip. No wooden-banked walls have to be jumped—you can probably putt the shot. (This maxim holds good with the majority of short holes anywhere, and goes well with Bobby Jones's idea of taking the easy shot with the stronger club.)

Anyone who gets his five 3's in the round is going to be desperately hard to beat.

The Final of the Putter takes place on the Sunday afternoon and were the finalists to adopt American methods no final would beat the onset of dusk. In 1926 the final between Wethered and Storey had to be abandoned at the 24th and both balls were hung on the Putter; in 1950, had Martin not beaten Lucas at the 23rd, the same must have happened. Golf also begins at dawn in the early rounds and the first tee at 8 a.m. of a January morning is no laughing matter—or should not be, yet laughter is the constant of this meeting—perhaps the last remaining competition which is played by the vast majority of the entrants for the fun of the game.

In the *Ballade of the Links of Rye*, written by John Somerville in 1898, occurs this verse:

How gay the heart is and how light
Where Beauty, Sport, and Friendship greet!
Where all the joys of life invite,
And warm it with their genial heat!
Sweet is the lark's song—but more sweet
The golfball's whistle as it flies
Swift t'ward the mark which it should meet—
The golfer lives in Paradise.

The views across to Rye Harbour and the Brede valley, with Camber Castle lying like a stranded ship in the middle; the sight of Rye itself, so foreign-looking and conical upon its hill; and across the bay, the great lion's paw of Fairlight Cliff holding down the sea—all these are beautiful. I will not say there are not greater links than Rye, but I will say and stick to it—that there are few which combine and gather into one place so many of those qualities which make the game of golf unique:

O fools! who drudge from morn till night
And dream your way of life is wise,
Come hither! prove a happier plight,
The golfer lives in Paradise!

SCORE CARD

Hole	Yards	S.S.S.	Hole	Yards	S.S.S.
1	465	5	10	325	4
2	185	3	11	350	4
3	455	5	12	430	4
4	430	4	13	435	5
5	175	3	14	185	3
6	485	5	15	440	5
7	163	3	16	430	5
8	430	4	17	235	3
9	320	4	18	435	5
Out	3108	36	In	3265	36
			Out	3108	36
			Total	6373	72

LOCAL RULES

1. *Out of Bounds:*
   (a) All ground north of the fence at the 1st, 2nd, 3rd, and 10th holes; and south of the fence at the 8th hole.
   (b) All enclosed ground, gardens, buildings, and the club premises.

2. *13th Hole.*—A ball driven from the tee, which lies within one club's length of the concrete wall, may be lifted and dropped, not nearer the hole, within two clubs' length, without penalty.

3. *Rabbit Scrapes, War Damage, Military Work.*—A ball lying in a rabbit scrape, war damage, or military work may be lifted and dropped, not nearer the hole, without penalty. If the ball lie in the rough, it must be dropped in the rough.

4. *Putting Green.*—If a ball lie on a putting green other than that to which the player is playing, it must be lifted and dropped, not nearer the hole, clear of the green.

ST. ANDREWS

Sweet saint whose spirit haunts the course
And broods o'er every hole,
And gives the Driver vital force
And calms the Putter's soul. . . .

THERE is nothing new to say about St. Andrews, just as there is nothing new to say about Shakespeare; but wherever in the world there is a natural masterpiece, critical man will try and "murder to dissect". The Old Course is dissected critically or uncritically with a vengeance! Fifty square feet—the size of a good big Board Room table—*fifty square feet* of divots are taken, roughly, every day. Not all are, alas, replaced. . . .

I must confess that I approached St. Andrews sceptically, and rather in the mood of the little girl in Landor's poem, seeing the sea for the first time:

all, around the child, await
Some exclamation of amazement wild.
She coldly said, her long lashed eyes abased,
Is this the mighty ocean? Is this all!

I hope she was converted. I arrived at St. Andrews by car from the south—a good way to arrive, for, coming over the hill, the University tower and the ruins of the Cathedral rise above a pastoral skyline before one sees the town—as do the heavenly towers of Chartres—and one's first glimpse is just these towers and beyond them the long stretch of white sand and sandhills, the sea, and in the far distance the north side of the Firth of Tay. One can imagine the Cathedral—it must have been superb in its prime —dominant on the rocky point, with the University under its wing, looking out north across the bay and north-west along that magnificent sand-beach to the point where the River Eden meets the sea. Geologists will tell you that at some remote time the sea receded from here, and that interaction of river and tide threw up sandbanks first; then, in time, "firm soil won of the watery main";

seeds carried on birds' feet; seeds wind-blown; vegetation knitting the sand together, coarse marram grass and rush at the sea's edge, bent and fescue withinsides. Whins—gorse to the southerner—came, and heather; and by the fourteenth century stretching north from the town was a long low tract of seaside heath, full of rabbits and foxes and ideal for hunting and archery practice.

It was only forty-odd years after the Battle of Agincourt that golf appears officially in history, in an Act of the Scottish Parliament, 1457. St. Andrews itself appears on January 25th, 1552. Archbishop Hamilton made a deed with the townspeople whereby the Church should farm the "cunningis" (rabbits) and the townspeople have the right "inter alia to play at golff, futball, schuting, at al gamis with all uther maner of pastyme as ever thai pleis". It is curiously apt that bad golfers should be called rabbits.

True that the Honourable Company of Edinburgh Golfers did, in fact, formulate the first rules of golf which St. Andrews copied ten years later, but the fact is that the Honourable Company was a small and select body amusing itself in a thriving capital city with a thousand other interests, while St. Andrews is a small homogeneous town, and once it had taken to golf it loved golf with single-hearted passion; and also it possessed, in its links, a supreme golfing terrain, which Leith was not. It was utterly natural for St. Andrews to become the genius of golf, and inevitable: life for its inhabitants thereafter was simple.

> *The tee, the start of youth, the game our life,*
> *The ball when fairly bunkered, man and wife.*

The first thing to do is to go out on to the links.

> *Is this the mighty Old Course? Is this all!*

No, from the very start one is aware of greatness and strangeness. Everyone has seen pictures of the first tee in front of the Royal and Ancient club house, but they give only a faint flavour of the scene as it is played ordinarily. Golf photographs are mostly like first-night audiences, they do not give an impression of the play. But golf has been running at St. Andrews for generations. There are the players ready to drive down the broad, wide, gently sloping expanse. Pedestrians begin to quicken across, accelerating like hens towards grain, either inland towards the houses or seaward towards the white rails that flank the right-hand side, making it rather like a race-course. Down the straight come these first shots.

> *Swift as a thought the ball obedient flies,*
> *Sings high in air and seems to cleave the skies,*

or else,

> *Along the green the ball confounded scours,*
> *No lofty flight the illsped stroke impowers.*

I feel that only verse should describe this initial blow, and what better than to extract from Thomas Mathison? Already the next party has moved into position:

> *Ardent they grasp the ball-compelling clubs,*
> *And stretch their arms t'attack the little globes.*

What is so marvellous about St. Andrews is that anyone can play upon any of its four courses. The Old Course is *not* exclusive; indeed golf upon it is non-stop in the season, and about eighty thousand rounds are played upon it in a year!

In July, August, and September you must ballot for a place on the tee the day before you intend to play. You put your name, and the time you would *like* to have, in the boxes (anyone in St. Andrews will explain this to you), a draw is made and times posted at various vantage-points in the town. If you had hoped for 9.50 and you get 11.45, well—you want to play? So you arrange your day accordingly and at the allotted hour, having bought your ticket—off you go, any one of you, to play what part you can on this Hamlet of all golf links.

Make no mistake: here is greatness and mystery and that strange element which is both real magic, sleight of hand, and a brilliant just keeping on "the windy side of the law". In the same way as Jupiter would descend as a swan or a bull or a shower of gold to gratify desire, or a Proteus in wrestling changed shape and form most alarmingly, so St. Andrews will employ every means to deceive, flatter, cajole, or dragoon you into loving it, and into admitting its mastery of *you*. Now, nobody who plays once or twice, or twenty or thirty times, will begin to *know* this links at all. That takes years or a lifetime.

But one thing is certain: it is unique, even at a first superficial glance. For it is a unique shape; rather like lesson one in learning knots, for it has a loop at the end round the 7th, 8th, 9th, 10th, and 11th and then returns the way it came: and, apart from the 1st, the 17th, and the 9th, all the greens are enormous double greens: thus 2 and 16, 3 and 15, 4 and 14, etc., are each a huge undulating putting surface; white outward flag, red homeward, waving in parallel like two terminals on a battery. This came about because in the early nineteenth century the course had only nine greens and you putted, both out and home, into the same hole; whoever arrived at the green first having precedence. But balls flying into your face became a menace even to the tough St. Andrews golfer, and by 1887 the course was roughly the shape and lay-out it is now. Incidentally, the cry of "Fore!" so feebly and apologetically crooned on English courses, has at St. Andrews its true fiery leonine value; and it has modulations elsewhere unknown. There is an intonation of Fore! to cover every contingency, and like Touchstone's seven forms of deceit, it has seven shades: there is the Fore courteous, the Fore mock-modest, the Fore churlish, the Fore valiant, the Fore quarrelsome, the Fore circumstantial, and the Fore direct. I have heard them all, the Fore direct being always in unison and terrible as the roaring of a bull.

Golf never stops on the Old Course, and lost balls must be left or you are immediately bumped. Also, golf is a very slow business between shots: a wait on every tee and for most second shots. That is, of course, in the summer season when soft is the sun. You will never have the course to yourself, but if you can brave the winter's rages you will play more quickly.

St. Andrews is colourful, for there is plenty of heather and whin to contend with (though not, of course, what it was). I think it is likely to surprise the newcomer how much heather there is. But you must remember that the Old Course is right up and down the middle of the long sea-heath and has both the New, the Jubilee, and the dunes between it and the North Sea, and upon its left flank it has the Eden Course, where once reposed the Elysian

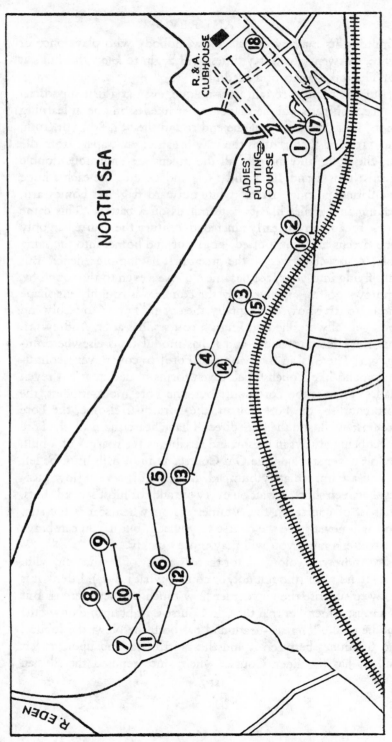

ST. ANDREWS—Plan of the course

fields. But never was a course so like the motions of the sea: the slow, steady start of the first four holes, the sudden stride of the long 'Hole o'Cross', this is just like the movement of the ebb—running quickly now through 'Heathery' to its farthest out, the 7th, the 'High Hole'. Now comes slack water in truth, for here is the loop and 8, 9, and 10 at flat, slack-water holes, to be exploited with all possible power. It is as if here at low water the old wreck shows its ribs, and one has *just* time to dig for the treasure in its hold before the tide turns again. No. 8 is short—the only outward short hole and a fairly easy 3; you can get 3's at the 9th and 10th too: and now as, just before it turns, the tide seems suddenly to recede a little farther and then begin to ripple inwards, now comes the short 11th. Its green pairs with the 7th but is a little farther out on the very edge of the links, so that a shot over the green seems as if it will drop splash! into the estuary of the Eden (and it nearly will; but, instead, will lodge in a hell of sand and marram grass). To guard the green—this end of it is tiny—there are two terribly cunning bunkers, 'Strath' for a slice and the 'Hill' for a pull. Get a 3 here and it is a pure gold doubloon. But Long John Silver's parrot may easily mock you with its cry, "Pieces of *eight*! Pieces of *eight*!" You *can* steal four 3's round the loop, you *should* take 3, 4, 4, 3, but . . . the incoming tide may float pieces of torn cards in with it.

From the twelfth tee to the eighteenth green, in floods the tide, and perhaps you are being lucky enough and playing well enough to come in with it till you reach the 'Road Hole', where the last sandcastle of your golfing pride and hope must stand against the waves until you are safely on the eighteenth tee. Many commentators have written about What Happens at the Road Hole in as erudite a fashion as Professor Dover Wilson's *What Happens in Hamlet*; yet like that great work of genius it survives all attempts to explain it. Mr. T. S. Eliot has said that *Hamlet*, as a play, is an artistic failure. Perhaps the Road Hole is, too.

But confronted with the magic of Old Course, and now with those black sheds that beetle o'er their base upon the tee, we are at a climax. The courageous or foolhardy cut across over them, the staid play safely leftward. Now the Road Hole is so called because exactly along the back edge of the narrow green, down a grassy sheer drop of three feet or so, *is* a road. It is necessary to remember that this road is *below* the level of the green; because it means that the recovery shot from the road surface, which is rough, bricky and cindery, and altogether horrible, must be *pitched* up on to the sliver of green and against the slope of it. What makes the player fall into this abyss? In the face of the green just left of centre is the Road bunker, so perfectly placed that it dominates play even from the tee, and by sheer force of its spidery personality drives its victims either to avoid it too carefully and chance the road, or play too safely, and so come into its parlour, and then, of course, a bunker shot just too well out will go into the road anyway. But what is the devil in the hole is its perfect length—you *can* get on in 2—you badly want a 4—and . . . but I am presuming upon too brief an acquaintance. I have no doubt all kinds of other subtle horrors have escaped my notice. But I must record the nice, mordant humour of another of its bunkers which lies between the 'Scholar's' bunker and the 'Road'—it is called the 'Progressing' bunker.

There are many named bunkers on the Old Course whose

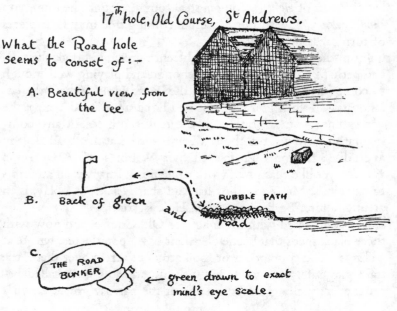

17ᵗʰ hole, Old Course, St Andrews.

What the Road hole seems to consist of :—

A. Beautiful view from the tee

B. Back of green and RUBBLE PATH road

C. THE ROAD BUNKER ← green drawn to exact mind's eye scale.

separate histories I wish I had time to discover, and relate. You must play many times before you can relish the real nicety of being in the 'Pulpit' or the 'Shell', the 'Cat's Trap' or the 'Lion's Mouth'; but coming to the 14th, with its famous bunker, I could not help recalling Dr. Faustus's question to Mephistophilis as to where Hell was, and Mephistophilis' answer:

Why this is hell, nor am I out of it. . . .

And it is strange to think that golf was being played over this ground when Marlowe's superb play first shocked and delighted Elizabethan audiences.

The decade of the 1890's was indeed the great decade of golf, as of so much else in English life. What a ten years! Taylor, Braid, and Vardon . . . Ibsen, Shaw, and Wilde . . . in 1897 the New Course was opened to relieve pressure on the Old. The New Course, next to the Old, is over the same kind of country of heather, whins, and dune, yet it is very, very different, and I do not think it should ever be compared with the Old. It is long, difficult and, yes, dull. Good, solid, testing golf, but I'm afraid I must repeat, a bit boring. I apologise to its staunch supporters and again I know that I do not know it well enough, but I feel that there is not very much to know. Pick it up and plump it on the other side of the bay by Leuchars aerodrome, and I rather doubt if it would be more than a longish holiday course, but I certainly recommend it as such.

In that year '97, too, the Royal and Ancient finally came to dominate, in fact, a world which it had ruled by right from time immemorial, for the Rules Committee was formed to legislate for the whole game, as it has done ever since. It was incidentally William IV, the Sailor King, who graciously permitted the title of 'Royal and Ancient'; and let us not forget that our present King is a past Captain of the club.

The William IV medal, that is the autumn medal, is perhaps the club's most treasured trophy, and one story concerning it cannot be left out.

Medal day in 1860 was a day of appalling gale and just as a certain Captain Maitland-Dougall, R.N., was about to start there

was a cry of "A wreck! A wreck! Man the Life-boat!" The life-
boat was launched, but there were not enough volunteers. The
gallant Captain downed his clubs, jumped aboard, and stroked the
boat to a successful rescue. At the end of which, hours later, wet,
sopping, and one would have thought exhausted, he returned to
the tee—and won the Medal!

But stories of golfing feats at St. Andrews are legion, and that
one must stand for all of them; legion also are the names of the
heroes: Old Tom and Young Tom, Allan Robertson, Andrew
Kirkaldy—it needs a Homeric touch to list them, and their deeds.

There is now a 'limited Sunday service' of golf at St. Andrews,
play being permitted upon the Eden Course, which, in character, is as far a cry from its neighbour as a play by J. B. Priestley
is from Shakespeare. But, in general, Sunday is a day for meditation—perhaps upon Mr. Eliot's summing up of the century we
live in:

> Their only monument the asphalt road
> And a thousand lost golf balls.

Perhaps it is a day for a little quiet putting on the drawing-room
carpet, or for finding some of those errant thousand, or even for
reading books about golf . . . certainly it is a day of expectancy; a
day on which—since we may not play on the Old Course—we
are all scratch players on it:

> Thou giv'st me to the world's last hour
> A golfer's fame divine;
> I boast—thy gift—a Driver's power,
> If I can Putt—'tis thine.

ST. ANDREWS

Hole	Name	Length	Hole	Name	Length
1	The Burn	374	10	Tenth	314
2	The Dyke	400	11	High	163
3	Cartgate	347	12	Heathery	316
4	The Ginger		13	Hile O'cross	409
	Beer Hole	424	14	Long	513
5	The Hole		15	Cartgate	404
	o'Cross	522	16	Corner of the	351
6	Heathery	370		Dyke	
7	High	354	17	Road	466
8	Short	153	18	Tom Morris	356
9	End	310			
				In	3292
	Out	3254		*Out*	3254
				Total	6546

Note.—There is not a fixed Standard Scratch Score for this course.

LOCAL RULES

1. *The Swilcan Burn.*—The portion of the Swilcan Burn running parallel to the fairway of the first hole and defined by white posts is a lateral water hazard. Rule 36 (3), applies.

2. *The 17th Hole (Old Course):*
   (a) Along the 17th fairway the grass between the Mussel Road and the wall is part of the hazard.
   (b) At the 17th green the bank leading down to the gravel footpath is not part of the hazard, but all the rest of the ground between the bank and the wall is part of the hazard.

3. *Obstructions.*—Drain covers, fixed seats, notice boards, boundary stones, posts and rope of the rope fences erected for championships or other golf tournaments are to be treated as immovable obstructions. Rule 33 applies.

4. *Out of Bounds:*
   (a) Beyond any wall or fence bounding the respective courses.
   (b) To the south of the Links Road.
      Note.—Beyond the fence bounding the Links Road, when it is erected.
   (c) Beyond any fences on the Ladies' Putting Links.
   (d) In any turf nursery.
   (e) In the garden adjoining the Shepherd's Cottage.
   (f) At the 17th hole Eden course—beyond the fence on the south side of the Mussel Road.
   (g) Beyond the white posts on the right of the 4th hole Eden Course.
   (h) On the beach beyond the sea wall at the 6th hole Eden course and beyond the white posts and/or boundary ditch on the left of the 12th and 13th fairways Eden course.

SUNNINGDALE

MANY people believe Sunningdale Old Course to be the finest inland golf course in England. I am among that number, but qualify the statement by saying, "Wait till the New Course is really in good order again"—as it will be by the time golfers read these words. The two courses are in great contrast. The Old Course winds among trees for most of its way. I do not mean that trees border the fairway, but that the course wears a loose cloak of trees and strides along freely in its heather-mixture within them. The New Course is open; a wild Spartan, utterly different from its neighbour. Only once does it take shelter; otherwise it is open-necked, tough, and athletic. I believe it will be a great course. I'm not trying to put supporters of the Old Course into a rage, no; but when both courses are there, if ever an inland champion-ship is to be played—here, I think, is the venue.

But to the Old Course: in 1926 the Open Championship was experimented upon. Its qualifying rounds were 'sectional' and the southern section was played at Sunningdale. And I must dwell upon this, for there was then played a round of medal golf the like of which has never been seen, and in going round Sunning-dale oneself it is fascinating to bear it in mind.

This round was played by Bobby Jones, then just coming to the zenith of his powers. It had 33 putts and 33 other shots: it had twelve 4's and six 3's, and it had one flaw. (In the next round he did a mere 68 to lead the qualifiers by 7 strokes.) I know that Norman Von Nida has done a 63 since then; but Jones's per-formance still seems to me as "incredible and indecent", as Mr. Darwin described it at the time.

As far as I can—with the help of his charming autobiography *Down the Fairway*—I want you to play that round with him.

The first hole is what first holes should be. It is long, gently downhill all the way, and quite wide enough: this is where the first difference between us mortals and Mr. Jones appears. He took a drive, a brassie, and two putts.

The prevailing wind is south-west, and it will be blowing from left to right across the second fairway. This is a nicely convex hole. The green is over the horizon from the tee, and it is *just* possible to be on in 2. It needs a long iron shot, or a spoon or No. 4 wood. Bobby Jones hit a No. 1 iron and took two putts. Sunningdale is a course perfectly suited to the long, accurate iron player.

The third hole is an extremely pretty hole. You drive across (I hope you do) a little heathery valley, and there are trees along the left to admire distantly. Two bunkers on the right-hand side of the fairway are placed exactly for the nervous cut; but this is a kindly drive-and-pitch hole and should be a certain 4. "Missed the putt for a 3", says Bobby.

The next hole is a short hole up a rather steep incline all the way. You have to hit a little farther than you think you have, but it is really rather a dull hole and you cannot see the bottom of the pin. "A mashie 25 feet from the pin and two putts" will do very nicely.

From the fifth tee a noble view appears. The sixth and seventh holes stretch out and away down the hill you have played up and away, away into the distance, in a long, slow sweep down-and-up-the-other-side.

"Conifer County of Surrey!" You suddenly realise how very well-wooded the course is, and at this moment the trees move quite perceptibly closer to the edge of the fairway. But from the fifth tee you feel comparatively free. One of the major pleasures of golf, surely, is driving from a tee perched up on a hill-side. The ball seems to soar and go on volplaning for ever like a gull; the hole seems to be miles away; and yet when you come down from the heights, it is not so far to the green after all! So the 5th is a delightful hole, and there is a watery grave short of the green on the right for the cut-and-run sort of second. Bobby Jones hit a No. 4 on to the outer confines of the green and slotted a long putt for a 3.

The 6th goes up the slope again, but gently, another two-shotter, and there is no possibility of a duffed second rolling home, rolling home. The fairway gives place to a belt of rough ridges, grassy and heathery, and over these you must go and pitch on, or only just short of the green. A drive and a No. 4 and two putts.

The 7th is a melodramatic hole. The hill-side rises sharply in front of the tee and you drive very blindly indeed over and down the other side into a defile of a fairway, a rather sinister green glen; and from this another No. 4 iron will reach the green. These three holes are each allotted four by 'Old Man Par, the imperturbable economist', and each demands an accurate second shot of about 150 yards.

The 8th is another short hole across a valley to a green jutting from the side of the slope and falling in a small grass cliff on its right flank. Don't cut here. Again, Mr. Jones's advice is well worth taking. "The others were using a mashie here. I used a No. 4 iron and an easy swing." There is, in fact, no short hole I know where that is not the best advice: take the stronger club and play it easy.

The 9th is a relaxable sort of hole. You can drive, or nearly drive, the green, and the fairway is flat and wide. From this fairway looking east, whence you have come, you suddenly realise that you have climbed quite steadily up and that the prospect pleases—even the prospect of the second 9. Bobby Jones overran the green with his drive, chipped back and missed the 5-foot putt, getting only a par 4. So out, 4, 4, 4, 3, 3, 4, 4, 3, 4 = 33, only one long putt holed.

If the tee shot from the 5th seems Alpine, this 10th is Himalayan, almost vertiginous. This hole will be a steady comfortable 5 for most people, and certainly more than a drive and a stiff No. 2 iron! The green is moving uphill on the other side of the valley and to reach home you need a long, long carrying shot.

I can't do better than quote the inexorable Jones for the next. "A blind drive with much grief if off line." Yes, there is! This is a dogleg to the right, the blindness is caused by a heathery ridge diagonally across, and there is an ocean of heather left or right. It is better to be a little left than right. If you can't be good, like Mr. Jones, be careful. The second shot is a pitch, and here he got a birdie 3.

The 12th is a lovely hole with a particularly tough second. The green is well up a hill-side and a bit dogleggy to the left, so that, again, the shot has to be hit long and accurately enough to carry all the way. Sunningdale has hardly been altered since Willie

SUNNINGDALE—Plan of the course

127

11th hole, Sunningdale

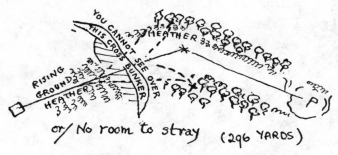

or/ No room to stray (296 YARDS)

Park laid it out in 1900, and there is no doubt at all that he chose his ground superbly, for though the heather had to be hacked up and burnt off and the fairways 'made', the thing about Sunningdale is that it seems such 'natural' golf. For an inland course this is a rare quality. From the hill-side above the twelfth green you play a dropping shot to the short 13th. It was here that Bobby J. made his "first mistake of the round; I think my only one". He actually cut his tee shot into a bunker! Naturally he chipped out and holed the putt for a 3, but still . . .

The 14th and 15th come out more into the open and are flat: the former is long: 500-odd yards, and as at the 1st, a drive and a brassie and two putts sufficed the Master. No. 15. 229 yards, par 3. "A driving-mashie 12 feet past the pin, well in line. Missed the putt."

This kind of long-short hole is perhaps the easiest of all kinds of holes to drop a stroke at. (The 17th at Rye is another.) Here, the hole is somehow 'just right' in its proportion to the last hole.

The last three holes finish 4, 4, 4, and so, of course, did Mr. Jones. They are very good holes too, and the 17th is precipitously down, the 18th grimly back up beside the first fairway and the green is ringed with bunkers as eager to display themselves as the diamonds on a newly engaged finger. Well, there we are. In, the score reads 4, 3, 4, 3, 4, 3, 4, 4, 4. "It's a wonderful course, Sunningdale, and I wish I could carry it about with me. . . ."

One shot in a bunker, otherwise a relentless easy accuracy. . . . The greens at Sunningdale are on the large side and beautifully true, and the silver-sand soil makes for crisp turf which is a joy to play from.

What is there about this Old Course? There is an extraordinary difference between those courses which have this over-all rhythm of play and those which have eighteen good separate holes. Muirfield is another place of perfectly balanced rhythm, and such courses seem able to draw golf out of you that you hardly knew was there, as a great conductor can from his orchestra.

But there is "much grief if off the line"—do not run away with the idea that Sunningdale is easy! There is trouble enough for the eccentric, and heather is a hazard you cannot get away with. Certainly it is not long, not a sheerly physical endurance test. It has a flavour all its own, a sweet austerity like a really good *vin rosé*. It is alive; it has retained, somehow, all the enthusiasm of its founders, in particular of Mr. J. A. Roberts whose portrait hangs in the club house. This sense of personality can be impressed upon a golf course as much as upon a house, and Sunningdale's personality is one of great energy and charm.

SUNNINGDALE

SCORE CARD

Holes	Yards	S.S.S.	Holes	Yards	S.S.S.
1	492	5	10	448	5
2	454	5	11	296	4
3	292	4	12	421	4
4	152	3	13	175	3
5	394	4	14	473	5
6	392	4	15	229	3
7	390	4	16	426	4
8	165	3	17	422	4
9	270	4	18	415	4
Out	3001	36	In	3305	36
			Out	3001	36
			Total	6306	72

LOCAL RULES

(Old Course. Match or Medal Play)

1. *Out of Bounds.*—All gardens adjoining both courses, and Flagstaff green on the left of the 18th green.

Note—Penalty: stroke and distance.

2. *Water Hazards.*—All ditches and the pond at the 5th hole on the old course must be treated as water hazards.

3. *Road crossing 2nd Hole on old course.*—A ball lying on or within one club's length of this road between the notice boards may be treated as on ground under repair.

4. *Ball on wrong Putting Green.*—A ball played on to a wrong putting green must be lifted and dropped without penalty as near as possible to the place where it lay, but not nearer the hole.

5. No path or road shall be deemed to be a hazard.

WALTON HEATH

To think of Walton Heath is to think of James Braid, that master of golf, who died, aged eighty, on November 27th, 1950. He had been at Walton Heath for over forty years, he *was* Walton Heath in a unique way. All golfers know or should know his record: his five championships; his innumerable other golfing honours; also his wisdom and skill as a golf architect. Latterly we all held our thumbs for those birthday rounds, when he went round in his age or less. I would like to record one small memory of him. It was at Royal St. George's at the championship of 1938, and I decided to follow him all the way round rather than mill in the crowds encompassing more recent heroes. He had only a modest gathering. But he gave us an exhibition of sheerly classical golf I shall never, never forget. Every shot was struck quite perfectly. He was then sixty-eight, and of the 'divine fury' of his driving only the divinity remained. But the ball seemed to go, somehow, straighter than straight; the second shots—often spoon shots against his partner's No. 6 irons—went plumb to the heart of the green, and the putting was utterly steady. Braid holed the links in 74, and the news that he was playing well spread, it seemed to me, not to the madding crowd but to fellow professionals. At any rate there seemed to be as many professionals as lay spectators round the home green, and they gave him their applause with a true respect and sincerity. Perhaps I am romancing, but the grand old man appeared to me to *blush*, and stumped off the green like a little boy who has just been given his colours. It was a most moving small incident, vivid in memory. It happened that I was at Walton the day after his death, and in a pub I heard a man say, "Yes, he must have been a *good* man . . . though I never saw him *play*", and that too seemed a fitting tribute.

Perhaps it is fanciful, but Walton Heath itself seems to be very like James Braid, for it is strong and modest, positive and forthright, yet never ostentatious. Walton Heath, by saying nothing, will give you its opinion of your golf. If you *ask* for an opinion you will get one and there will be no mincing matters. "There's likewise a wind on the heath. . . ." Yes, Walton is a real heath, six hundred feet up, a great wild expanse of bracken, heather, and thorn-trees. It has none of the birch-coloured charm of Sunningdale; it is wide open, and there always *is* a wind blowing across it. It seems to move with the long, slow, loping stride, never hurried, of its genius. Many people will know—and it hangs in the club house to see—the cartoon by Spy of the young Braid. A tall, lanky, angular figure, knees a little bent, back a little bent, head a little bowed, yet the whole giving an impression not of a drooping melancholy, but of a modest yet iron concentration and purpose. That, I think, is the character, too, of this grand golf course. It moves you along slowly and inexorably. It says, "Your business is to play round, not even stopping for lost balls—because you should hit straight; nor to admire the view—for your business is to concentrate. You are to keep going: golf is a game of flowing rhythm, of a steady resolve, it is not over till the ball is in the bottom of the hole and you have lost or won or put down your final score."

Even though the word has been done a mischief to, I must use it: Walton Heath is austere. But it lets you begin lightly enough. The first hole is in a little quiet backwater of its own. It is a drive and pitch, or run-up, and there is plenty of room. It gives you no hint of what is beyond its sheltering surround of trees. Through them you go, cross the road (and look out! It's dangerous), through the trees on the farther verge—and out on to the heath proper. From now on there is no shelter, no wind-break, and the thorn bushes only make the wind prick more keenly. This 2nd is a splendid hole. It is long; and about half-way, the fairway suddenly swoops down into a rough grassy, tussocky, defile; up the other side; and on again to the green. Your second shot, a full brassie, must be played across this gulf and on to the farther slope —a shot easy enough in itself, but a first-class mental test for a second hole. The third green can be driven, though it is all the way a just-uphill gradient. The 4th is very long and flat.

A remarkable feature of Walton is the way its bunkers—particularly those placed strategically in the fairway—rear their ramparts up. They are curiously, aggressively, artificial looking.

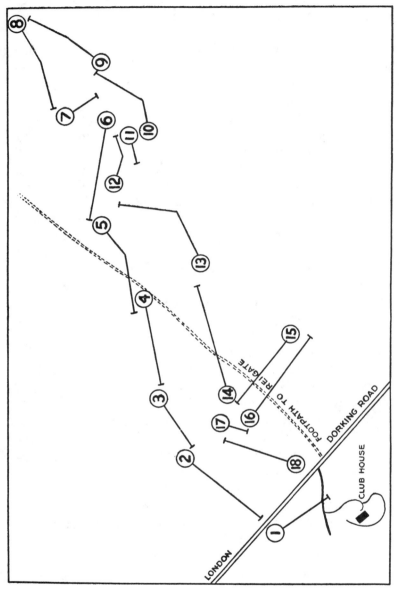

WALTON HEATH—Plan of the course

That may be another way of saying they're old-fashioned, but I am glad to see that they have not been reduced in height or blended more with the landscape. They are uncompromisingly BUNKERS. You cannot make the excuse, "I never knew it was there". These bunkers are positive, direct, and need make no comment upon such as enter them. Another thing, too, about the 3rd and 4th (and it is true of the 6th and 8th) is that they are particularly *straight* holes. Their straightness is challenging. It bets you, from the moment you tee your ball, that you just can't hit as straight as *that*! For straightness has degrees, however paradoxical that may sound, and these holes demand an absolute, Platonic, straightness. It is not until you reach the 5th that you will have a long iron shot to play. Here you drive downhill towards a curving shoulder of fairway on the right which will shrug your ball off into bunkers along the left like a spiv declining a bad bargain. If you place your drive correctly there's a long iron shot home to a green nibbled round most of its perimeter with bunkers. This seems to me to be a particularly good two-shotter. In its remorseless way Walton then says, "You may have done it once, let's see if you can do it again"—and presents you with another hole of almost the same length. This is one of the arrow-straight kind with nothing to stop you but your own inefficiency. You can, in a very literal sense, always see what you are doing on these first nine holes. Aberrations can be measured by degrees. (A is 7 degrees to the right of the exact line; B is 15 degrees, so he is in the playable heather; C is 17 degrees and in heather and bracken a foot high.) Not that Walton is appallingly narrow—I've known fairways half the width which still look safe and probable landing-grounds—but the proportions of carry-from-the-tee, and rough, and deep rough, to the length of the hole make the course seem narrow, and the bunkers shrink the fairways like laundries.

The 7th is a short hole, and not a very memorable one; rather a sustainer of the general level than anything else. It is long enough, however, not to be an easy breathing-space, and I should think more 4's are shot there than 3's, and it is the only short hole going out.

Before leaving the rough I must recall that when we visited Walton from Cambridge I remember James Braid saying on the first tee, as he started our match, "If you can't take your spoon, take your niblick". No more need now be said about the rough. The 8th is another William Tell kind of hole, direct and straight as a guardsman, and it takes you to the farthest point of the course.

Turning back for the 9th, there comes a series of five excellent holes of a rather different character. To continue the military metaphor, these next five stand-at-ease, or stand-easy, though they are by no means so easy to play. The 10th immediately introduces a new element; it is really doggy-leggy. You drive to the lip of a little valley, and round the bend to the right on the opposite slope is the green. It's an uphill across-the-valley second, which mustn't be cut, but the point is that this is a rather picturesque, attractive-looking hole, and it comes as a welcome change. It is followed by another short hole, back over the valley which is now full of heather, and at the end of a gently rising slope the other side is the green—quite far enough away at that. The 12th proceeds in an enchanting right-handed arc; yes, it's a curving hole rather than an angular one. The fairway banks round like a motor-race-track, and crossing it half-way is a raised-up road, which acts as a sort of elevator for your second. I mean that it helps you to hit the ball in the air, which you should do anyway. You con-

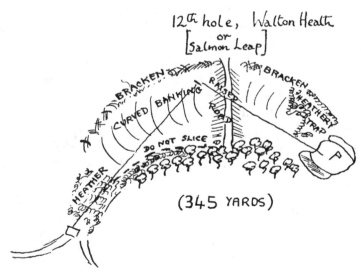

12ᵗʰ hole, Walton Heath
[or Salmon Leap]

BRACKEN BRACKEN
CURVED BANKING RAISED HEATHER TRAP
DO NOT SLICE
HEATHER
P

(345 YARDS)

tinue on a curving course at the next. You drive to the crest of a hill (and don't top here, the heather is jungle-thick in front of the tee), and having reached it, the hole is seen to be miles away round to the right—and you can, if you dare, cut the corner.

This is the end of the relaxation period. You are called to attention and will be inspected over the last five. The 14th starts you off with another long, long, straight bogey 5. The 15th is another of those long two-shot holes with menacing bunkers which look like the earthworks of some vanished tribe. Incidentally the 16th returns parallel, and this is the only occasion where the slicer can exchange fairways and get away with it. After two shots at this 16th you will find yourself with a steep uphill pitch to a green on a shelf with a sheer drop to the right and a yawning bunker there to catch the shot that is in the least feeble and cut away. It needs a very skilful *polished* kind of approach; nothing slipshod will do. It is that moment when the Inspecting Officer stops in front of you, and looks you up and down . . . and . . . If you pass, the short 17th is almost a relief: it goes across a deep gully of heather and thorn to a green exactly on the farther side. This is not a hole of great distinction, but it is attractive enough and a not-too-easy 3. The last hole has a really large old-fashioned cross-bunker guarding the whole green; one of those bunkers with little scaling ladders at intervals which make me think of mediaeval sieges, and defenders with pots of boiling oil at the top. If you get into this bunker I am sure you will pour the boiling oil of rage and despair on your own head. So near home, and then—hack, hack, hack. . . . Did I not say that Walton Heath never relaxes till the ball is in the last hole?

It would not be right to leave the place without celebrating its architect, Herbert Fowler, for this is a truly splendid test of the game, and the New Course, which runs over the same tract of land, mostly to the north-west of the Old, is very little behind it in quality.

The whole of the soil is loam, with the chalk twenty-odd feet below, and this means that it is always dry. The turf is close, almost seaside in texture, and the ball needs to be hit very truly; it never sits up and begs. You've got to play golf here—'and no error', as they say.

WALTON HEATH

SCORE CARD

Hole	Length	S.S.S.	Hole	Length	S.S.S.
1	300	4	10	425	4
2	445	4	11	175	3
3	285	4	12	345	4
4	455	5	13	490	5
5	395	4	14	575	5
6	400	4	15	390	4
7	170	3	16	478	5
8	470	5	17	167	3
9	420	4	18	410	4
Out	3340	37	In	3455	37
			Out	3340	37
			Total	6795	74

LOCAL RULES

1. *Rabbit Scrapes.*—A ball lying in a rabbit scrape may be lifted and dropped, or on the putting green placed, as near as possible to the place where it lay, but not nearer the hole, without penalty. A ball lying in a hazard must be dropped in the hazard.

2. *Ground Damaged by Horses.*—A ball lying on the fairway or putting green on ground damaged by horses may be lifted and dropped, or on the putting green placed, as near as possible to the place where it lay, but not nearer the hole, without penalty.

3. *Road, 12th Hole.*—A ball lying on or within a club's length of that part of the road within the limits of the fairway at the 12th hole may be lifted and dropped behind without penalty.

Note.—(*a*) The track of the gallop crossing the 13th and 16th fairways is 'ground damaged by horses'.

(*b*) The 'fairway' shall be taken to mean that part of the Course which is specially prepared for play by cutting and rolling.

137

WESTWARD HO!
Royal North Devon

———————◇———————

THE Royal North Devon Golf Club is the oldest seaside links in England, and it has remained, to this day, very much as it began: as its greatest of great golfers, J. H. Taylor, said to this writer in 1950, "the finest natural golf links in the world". It has therefore grown progressively more strange to successive generations of successively more 'artificial' golfers. R. C. Robertson-Glasgow has written of cricket "that the English cricket called First-class is sophisticated almost to death. Sometimes it seems that we have been playing this game of cricket far too long. . . ."

His thesis is that courage and daring have been driven out by caution, correctitude, and the fear of making mistakes. In the same way a child segregated and refined in upbringing to the nth degree of hygiene falls a helpless victim to the first germ it meets in the outside world; its red corpuscles appeal to the Minister of Health instead of getting on with repelling the invader.

But Westward Ho! was a wild and rough child and has grown to a hardy, healthy, weather-defying old age; it hasn't lost a tooth.

The links is on common land and cows, sheep, and horses are grazed on it; leaving their inevitable traces and doing steady but sporadic damage. The 'modern' professional or amateur will not quite enjoy playing here, because he will not be flattered. He will find that it is very difficult to break 80, and he will, I suspect, hint that the links is 'unfair' rather than admit his own shortcomings.

One can foresee a time, in golf, when the preparation of the greens for a competition will not be left to the local greenkeeper, but will be muddled out by an international committee of Absentee Experts, just as now in cricket the preparation of the Test wicket, it is felt, should not be left to the mere caprice of the man on the spot, who naturally does not know how to do the job. Natural wickets and natural golf: perhaps before long there will be a sudden swing from the over-prepared to the wild:

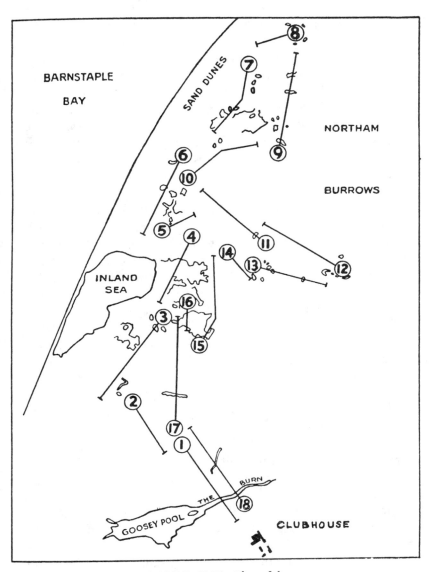

WESTWARD HO!—Plan of the course

professionals—and the public—will get bored with 63's and 64's; they will hold a meeting at Westward Ho! which will be won in a score considerably over 4's, say 78 and 81 and 74 and 79, and will turn to one another and say, "Why, *this* is the very thing—how clever we are to have discovered this beautiful and antique place". Perhaps they will rush to encase their concrete club-house walls with genuine old corrugated iron, and even have false sheaths of plastic material made to look like hickory over their supersonic steel shafts. Perhaps . . . And they will still find that the winds blow free and that green grow the rushes-o!

These superb sheaves of rushes are unique to this place, so far as I know. They stand up to the shoulder thick and bushy like clumps of gigantic shaving brushes; they are mildly poison-tipped, and you may have to question which is the worse: to get into them, or to get them into you. Around and about among them weave a race of furtive men whose dogs, more efficient than any radioactive detector, may find your lost ball; or have their masters impounded it in a kind of—shall I say—pocket limbo?

"The best golf links are to be found," wrote Horace Hutchinson, "at the mouths of rivers." Until the war destroyed it, there used to be links on both sides of the estuary; Saunton on the north, Westward Ho! to the south. Saunton was a fine links but it had none of the crusty, obstinate character of this place "providence clearly intended to be a golf links", as one of its originators remarked.

What is curious about this links is that it has a prologue and an epilogue. Sometimes, I remember, in the school chapel, we used to sing the longer hymns first two . . . and last two verses only; but there were always dreamers who carried on to verse three instead of jumping. If one played first two and last two holes only at Westward Ho! one would get no idea at all of what the links was; what it *meant*—any more than we boys paid the slightest attention to the theological arguments so rudely cut short in the hymns.

The first two holes are straight, wide, and flat, and go straight out towards the sea. Along the right-hand side of the 1st, runs a sort of Hoylake 'cop', but not close enough to the line to be more directly menacing than a first Income Tax demand.

Along the left are little, ordinary, pliable lilliputian rushes; there to mock you in memory as you meet their Brobdingnagian cousins. They are called 'fog' (pronounced 'fug'), and though they may impede your pilgrimage do not unduly daunt the soul. Then on the third tee you turn at right angles to the pebble-ridge and see ahead the sandhills and the First Act of the real links. The next six holes among the dunes are perfect golf holes, happy holes with only here and there violent horrors which may hint at the change of theme in Act II. For example, there is a vast wooden-walled bunker to be driven over, the 4th—a carry of about 150 yards—and at the 7th a snatch of the grand rush theme (if I may change my simile from drama to music) to the left of the line.

The sixth hole, from a tee perched up in the sandhills, is a superb two-shot hole. The drive is a gentle down-gradient to the hummocky fairway which slopes down with a tilt to the right. This fairway is like a large old-mole-hill field and an uneven lie or stance is certain for your second, which must ascend again, to a small green naturally shelving out of the dunes, and taking your ball more quickly from left to right than you might expect. From the sixth tee you also see the real shape of the links—and the shape of things to come.

You can see how the estuary coils its way inland with Apple-dore on the last bend, and to the right of Appledore, Northam, on the hill-side, where the great J. H. Taylor was born.

The sixth tee is where, once for all, you realise there is no turning back. You have been given a generous start. You have had a 3 at the short 5th; now, until suddenly the links relaxes its grip at the long 13th, every shot will tell: not only straightly struck but placed with care. This high sixth tee—the only real view of the sea—is the moment when a fierce prosecuting wind gets in a first deadly question and you falter a little before you answer: the answer may be a good one—but Judge Par noticed and your own counsel's heart missed a beat.

Turning inland upon the ninth tee the curtain goes up on Act II—9th, 10th, 11th, and 12th.

The rushes! But there's plenty of room for your drive on the right. This 9th is not difficult; it is a kind introduction to the tenth tee, where you take arms and your driver against a sea of

6ᵗʰ hole, Westward Ho!
(414 YARDS)

Seen from behind second shot

troubles. You must drive right over the rushes, and the farther left you carry over them the better, for the hole is doglegged left and a really long drive will whizz bravely over them, like an airman over the upraised spears of a warlike tribe; so far two slightly cut drives at these two holes will serve the cautious. But on the eleventh tee one must simply hit straight, over rushes and between rushes that line the fairway grimly like a hostile crowd held still only by fear of reprisals. Among them weave the very-plain-clothes detectives searching for balls as if they were bombs.

At the 12th, again, there are masses of room to the right; and the rushes are passed "and it's daylight at last".

What makes these rushes a unique and formidable hazard is that they are, simply, unplayable. There is no rough: there is fairway or disaster, and even the leniency of the present rule (as I write) does not really annul their horrifying powers on the mind. For truly, even in the wind, there *is* quite a lot of room; always enough, and were they simple 'fog' they would be as nothing. They are a mental hazard of supreme quality. For they are exactly the right size to inspire the maximum of unrest: larger, and one would be hopelessly resigned or turn on them in defiance; smaller, and one would not fear them.

The 13th, a wide, long, pleasant bogey 5 which one can reach in two good shots, is the perfect anodyne.

The rushes give a last snarl at the short 14th, for you can top a shot at a short hole just as easily as at any other.

The 15th is a beautiful two-shot hole almost right-angled; and with one strange phenomenon, an entirely artificial bunker beside the green, rearing a built-up façade which looks quite ridiculous:

it is necessary though, as a sand-break, or the wind would blow the sand out of the bunker on to the green: the bunker, too, is really necessary—though your journey into it is not. The 16th is a short hole in the great class—deceptively easy and with a duck's back of a green off which your ball rolls like a waterbead.

That is the end of the play, but the epilogue remains; the 17th and 18th return straight inland, as the 1st and 2nd went seaward across the flat grazing country. The 17th is very long and the 18th —just as you think you're quite safe—presents the last twist of the knife. All across the front of the green runs a muddy ditch— euphemistically called a burn—where the more marine-minded ball-hunters probe in the opaque coffee-coloured slop with rakes. Medal cards have been wrecked here within sight of the shore. The only man ever to break 70 in competition is the Hon. Michael Scott. But many hearts have been broken in the attempt.

WESTWARD HO!

Holes	Length	S.S.S.	Holes	Length	S.S.S.
1	450	5	10	361	4
2	419	4	11	372	4
3	415	4	12	425	4
4	352	4	13	440	5
5	139	3	14	182	3
6	414	4	15	399	4
7	392	4	16	145	3
8	199	3	17	551	5
9	471	5	18	416	4
Out	3251	36	In	3291	36
			Out	3251	36
			Total	6542	72

LOCAL RULES

1. *Extent of Hazards.*—The following are hazards:
(*a*) the great sea rushes, with the exception of the grass growing therein;
(*b*) all ditches on the course, to the level of the surrounding ground, and whether there be water lying in them or not, are water hazards;
(*c*) metalled roads. The following are not hazards: (*a*) the small rushes, locally known as 'fog', (*b*) permanent grass in a bunker.

2. *Great Sea Rushes.*—If a ball lie, or be lost, in the great sea rushes, a ball may be dropped, under penalty of one stroke (*a*) where a clear swing can be obtained, (*b*) not nearer the hole, (*c*) behind the spot at which the original ball pitched into the rushes, or (*d*) behind similar rushes as nearly as possible in line with that spot.

3. *Ditches.*—When dropping from a ditch the ditch will, in all cases, be kept between the player and the hole.

4. *Timber in Bunkers.*—A ball lying within two clubs' length of the timber facing of any bunker may be lifted and dropped, without penalty, in the bunker, two clubs' length from the timber.

5. *Free Drops.*—A ball lying in (*a*) a rabbit hole or scrape, (*b*) in a cart track, sheep track or tank trap, (*c*) in, or so near to that it interferes with the player's stance or swing, any military work or military fencing, may be lifted and dropped, without penalty, not nearer the hole. If on the green the ball will be placed.

6. *Side Greens.*—A ball lying on a putting green other than that of the hole being played must be lifted and dropped, without penalty, on the course, as near as possible to the place where it lay, but not nearer the hole.

7. *Immovable Objects.*—For the purposes of Rule 11 (general) all shelters, huts, telephone poles, and their stays, and wooden steps over bunkers are deemed immovable.

144

WORLINGTON AND NEWMARKET
Royal

———————◇———————

THE Royal Worlington and Newmarket Golf Club, by Hand of Genius out of Dispensation of Nature, took shape and form in 1891. If ever there was a classical golf course this is it. Here is really Greek-tragedy golf; an experience to purge the spirit and leave one humble, yet without rancour. Classical but also romantic, like a great, unfortunate, love-affair:

> *Age cannot wither her nor custom stale*
> *Her infinite variety.*

Yes, this is a Cleopatra among courses and it demands a mature and all-for-love Antony to conquer it, and to count the world well lost. Here, at the height of his fame, might some great amateur retire, disappearing like a meteor, to devote a lustrum mastering the tee shot to the 5th; another to the approach to the 4th. And yet, finally, the rewards of this unique course are intellectual and not sensual; here the golfer learns, if he is ever to learn, wisdom and philosophy. μηδὲν ἄγαν, *Aurea mediocritas*, nothing to excess, the golden mean: the rewards of keeping straight for every single shot. Fittingly, it is here that generations of Cambridge undergraduates have first tested their powers against the Ideal of Golf; here that so many have found out the superficiality and falseness of those adolescent golf courses on which they have been accounted skilful. There is no escape at Mildenhall. The course is ruthless and unforgiving. Yet, at a first glance, it looks innocent, flat, wide; and you go twice round. What could be easier? If ever a man declares, "Nine holes are not enough: real golf requires eighteen", let him be reminded of Mildenhall: for there is no more difficult feat of real golf in this country; probably anywhere in the world.

Mildenhall has the geological luck to lie upon a thin belt of perfect sand which runs through Norfolk, like a golf-stream. The sand in the bunkers is the colour of the advertiser's "rich golden brown" of patent breakfast-food, and it is as difficult to take clean as such foods are without milk and sugar, which is not here provided. The turf through the green has all the quality, without the looseness of texture, of seaside turf: it is dry and springy but more closely knit and it holds the ball without favour—it has the sense of a first-rate prose style—direct, without frills, yet without concessions, with certain quirks of mordant wit, but over-all with a wonderful fluency and power. You replace turf with respect. Several notices tell you to do so. This is no place for the golfing spiv.

The greens are sheer poetry:

> *My myne of precious stones, my emperie,*
> *How blest am I in thus discovering thee!*
> *To enter in these bonds is to be free. . . .*

It is no use imagining that even an indifferent putt will do. If you have the freedom of the greens at Mildenhall you know how to putt: you can putt anywhere. There seems to be a consistency of soil here which is unyielding, hard yet viable. The feel to the foot is unlike anywhere else. Some of the secret, again, is this seaside-ness-found-inland—yes, the greens here are like swimming in a mountain lake, as compared with the sea. The lake water is clear-cold—you can see to the bottom; and it is unresilient, not buoyant as salt. On good seaside greens you still get a sea-quality—one's ball *is* buoyant, it floats, if you are putting well, and sometimes reaches the bottom of the hole on a line you do not see. At Mildenhall, never. A belly-flopper of an approach will not do. The approach must be clean, the putt perfectly timed and struck: then the reward—to stand and watch, *with certainty*, the long putt going home to the bottom—a marvellous clear-water feeling. I know of no other greens that are so utterly scrupulous. Putting upon them is a sheer aesthetic delight—in one's own skill pitted against the best of the greenkeeper's. If Plato had played golf, here was the place for him Ideally to Putt.

Mildenhall's nine diamonds need playing; need all the cutter's art to become brilliants—make no mistake, they have as many

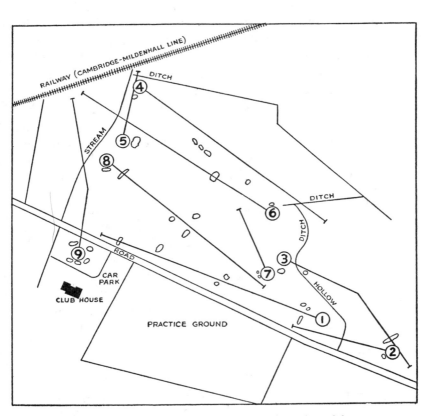

WORLINGTON AND NEWMARKET—Plan of the course

147

facets, highlights and angles as any diamond, and they are quite as hard.

I can only contrive to suggest settings. Of the first hole it is easiest to say that you will be surprised and even irritated to find you have taken 6. I cannot see why you should have. Wait till it becomes the 10th. The 2nd is a long one-shot hole—a brassie or spoon as often as not. The first time I played (as an undergraduate) it was with a Welsh contemporary, "My God," he said, "it is like pitching on a policeman's helmet." It is. You will take 4 here more often than 3. There is no trouble save a bunker on the right where the copper's ear would be. It will be deaf to your protestations. "But, officer, I was only *just* the wrong side of the white line. . . ."

At the 3rd you drive over that glorious old-fashioned obstacle a cross-bunker; at least you ought to. The fairway is a slightly convex ridge and all along the left it falls away into a grassy ditch which curls left, then right, like a left-handed question mark Ϛ, with the green just over the curve at an angle leftwards to the fairway. This is one of the best two-shot holes in the world, for this green is perfectly and subtly set, bunkered on its left edge and nothing but a long straight drive will give you pause for even a slightly imperfectly struck second. Down to the left in the ditch you will drag your slow length along like Pope's wounded snake and reach the green in 3, or even 4. Along the right, wide of the rough—so wide ?—are fir-trees, and hawthorn thickets; along the right, too, for a long drive, is a grassy hollow marish-ground where the lies are low. A 4 here, including two putts, is always good golf. Now come to the fourth tee. The scene changes; the minor characters go off: the next three holes will reveal the heart of the plot; the view is suitable. From this tee you look into a Grimm's faery land. On your right a hundred yards away a dark fir-plantation stretches off, curving tactfully to allow your slice as much latitude as the trolls will permit. To the left stands a clump of four sentinel firs where the short-cutting caddies wait. Beyond, and half-left of them, stretches away another long double line of firs, well away for this fourth hole; but there it is, a long Doric temple.

Framed in this dark opening V will be the 4th, 5th, and 6th, the

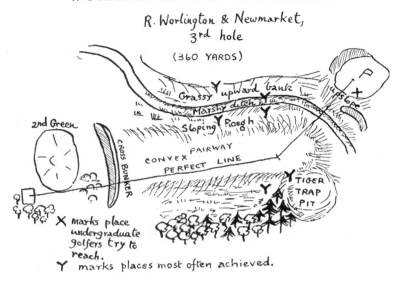

R. Worlington & Newmarket,
3rd hole

(360 YARDS)

2nd Green

Grassy upward bank

Marshy ditch

Sloping Rough

CROSS BUNKER

CONVEX FAIRWAY PERFECT LINE

TIGER TRAP PIT

X marks place
undergraduate
golfers try to
reach.

Y marks places most often achieved.

4th being in the right-hand stroke of the V. There are masses of
room; but a drive too much left will catch a long rampart of a
bunker and your shot out will probably catch one of a chain
of pot-bunkers placed there like beggars' palms for such a
pilgrimage.

The fourth fairway modulates and undulates away, narrowing
to a green which is just over the last round curving swell of
ground. Along its right, striking inward, is a watery dyke: at its
back, after only a few feet of rough, a wire fence, so that the
player is now hitting into the point of an inverted $\wedge$, and he must
pitch his long second exactly on the last upsloping inch so that it
may check, yet persevere, or he may play short and then have
his convex third scuttling over the green like a late politician
scuttling for the lobby on a vote he-knows-not-what. There is a
mediaeval-looking instrument for recovering your ball from the
dyke.

Now for the short 5th. A superb hole. Played at right angles
across the fourth green you are aiming straight for the end of the
fir-tree colonnade. The green lies just under it—a devilish creature,
a very Caliban of a green. It, too, is convex in its upper slopes, falls
suddenly, sharply, half-way and at this near end to us from the tee

149

it has a small saucer-like portion where the hole is cut, I imagine, once a year, on the greenkeeper's birthday.

There are no bunkers on this hole—nor need of them. To the left of it is a deep grassy pit (once full of water), out of which it is *possible* to stay on the green, but only by an exquisite piece of skill and fortune: to the right a stiff slope down into the rough and into the stream which, all along the right, beckons its way.

If you hit on to the green, into the saucer (and the pin is on the upper half of the green), you are faced with a putt as nearly perpendicular as you are ever likely to see. If you go right, or left, we will leave you ping-ponging away for a 6; for we have hit the perfect tee shot; starting a shade right, with a draw, pitching at the bottom right hand of the saucer and spinning up the slope to the flag. Your shot, Mr. Cotton. After you, Mr. Locke. On competition days the pin is often put right at the top of the green under the trees, and with the wind against you may need a No. 2 iron in order to find the pit; but often a No. 6 will do.

The sixth hole goes all the length of the fir-colonnade, along its left. The green is just angled—right, round the end of it—so deftly that you cut your second, for no reason but thinking of that angle, into the trees. The approach to the green has a subtle and trapping ridge which turns your ball off the green like a park-keeper chasing an urchin.

Now we are out of the wood and the short 7th has only to be hit straight. But the cunning release from claustrophobia tends to make you short, or slice into one of three bunkers you can't quite see, or hook into another which is larger than you thought. This is the easiest hole on the course. The 8th is a long hole with a lovely second over another cross-bunker down a slope to a green tucked under the trees exactly the other side from the 5th. The whole left-hand side of the green is bunkered, the bunker greedily ending on the near side with a bite into the green, which will pick up a shot only just left of the flag.

The 9th is a slight dogleg to the right. You must decide how much of the stream which runs along the right you can carry, or you will be out of bounds. A pitch over the road gets you home to the green and the club house is beckoning beyond, but now, now, with all your good and bad shots in your mind *you must go round again.* Psychologically, nine-hole golf is extremely different from the turn on an eighteen-holer, and the club house is a very attractive one—an old farmhouse with stone and brick floors and a thatched roof.

I would very much like to see, here, a small invitation tournament for, say, twenty of the best players in the world. I think they would be surprised at their scores: the record for the nine holes is —fantastically—28 shots: the competition record for the eighteen is 70. At full stretch in winter I myself very much doubt if the golf chronicler would have to stick together the bits of many broken 70's.

WORLINGTON AND NEWMARKET

SCORE CARD

Hole	Length	S.S.S.	Hole	Length	S.S.S.
1	484	5	10	484	5
2	242	3	11	242	3
3	360	4	12	360	4
4	480	5	13	480	5
5	152	3	14	152	3
6	435	5	15	435	5
7	162	3	16	162	3
8	459	5	17	459	5
9	300	4	18	300	4
Out	3074	37	In	3074	37
			Out	3074	37
			Total	6148	74

Note.—The Standard Scratch Score has now been fixed at 72, but the bogey of the course is being left at 74.

LOCAL RULES

1. *Out of Bounds:*
   (a) Over the road at the 1st and 2nd holes.
   (b) In or over the ditch on the right of the 4th green.
   (c) In or over the stream on the right going to the 5th.
   (d) To the right of the posts from the 9th tee to the stream and in or over the stream beyond the post by the first tree.
   (e) Beyond the line of posts or through the fence at the back of the 9th green.
   (f) Beyond the permanent wire at the back of the 4th green.
   Penalty—stroke and distance.

2. *Ditches and Streams.*—A ball in the portion of the stream at the 9th that is not out of bounds can be lifted and dropped on the side farthest from the hole, within two clubs' length, under penalty of one stroke. The ball must be played opposite the spot where it entered the stream.
   A ball played into any other ditch can be lifted and dropped behind, within two clubs' length, under the penalty of one stroke.

3. *Permanent Wire or Fence.*—A ball lying so near to permanent wire or fence as to interfere with the playing of the next stroke may be lifted and dropped within two clubs' length, but not nearer the hole, under the penalty of one stroke.
   In the case of the wire at the back of the 4th green, however, it must be dropped within one club's length and may be nearer the hole. The penalty is one stroke.

4. *Rabbit Scrapes.*—A ball lying in a rabbit scrape on the fairway may be lifted and dropped behind, as near as possible to the scrape, without penalty.

5. *Putting Greens.*—A ball lying on any putting green other than the one being played to must be lifted and dropped to the edge of the green to which it lies nearest, but not nearer the hole being played to. If a hazard intervenes in the line of play the ball must be dropped so that the hazard still remains in the line of play. The ball may, however, be played as it lies with a putter.

6. *Cleaning a Ball on the Putting Green.*—A ball lying on the prepared surface of a putting green can be lifted and cleaned and replaced on the same spot without penalty.

APPENDIX

I HOPE the notes which follow may be of use to golfers. I would like to emphasise that the lists of hotels may not be complete, nor are they in any order of merit. I never recommend the books I like even to my friends: even less would I recommend them strange food and drink. Golfers are on the whole cautious and shrewd. They walk forward to see the line. I think in planning a holiday one should reconnoitre as much as is possible by post, gossip, bush telegraph, and any other means, but it is something to do oneself. Wherever I stayed myself I was very comfortable. Let us leave it at that.

As to the information about the actual golf clubs, I beg secretaries to forgive me for any inaccuracies that may have crept into my notes. Give me a short putt or two on the way round!

ABERDOVEY

Once at Aberdovey there is no need for a car. The entrance to the links is not easy to find. Aim for the railway station and all is well.

The Trefeddian Hotel overlooks the links.

Other hotels in the town are: The Dovey; Pen Helig; Cwm Awel.

Green fees, July, August, and September: 7s. 6d. a day; 15s. 6d. a weekend; 30s. a week; 63s. a month. Reduced fees in winter.

No introduction is necessary.

Tea only.

CARNOUSTIE

The two courses are owned by the town. It is the Championship course that you will want to play on first of all.

It is nearly always possible to arrive and start save at weekends, but it is advisable to book a starting-time. Starter's box, tel. 3249. Few people seem to play in the afternoons. In summer everybody in Carnoustie plays after tea till dark. The chance one-round visitor is advised to aim at a 1.30 start.

By train or bus from Dundee the journey takes about forty minutes.

There is no food or drink to be had at the course itself: it must be got in hotel or café.

The Bruce Hotel; The Glencoe Hotel; The Kinloch Arms; Morven Hotel (Private); Panmuirbank Bank (Private).

No Sunday play on Championship course. Sunday play on Burnside course.

Green fees, *Championship:* 3s. 6d. a round; 6s. a day; 20s. a week; £2 a month. *Burnside:* 2s. a round; 10s. a week; 30s. a month. Remember to keep your green-fee ticket. You may be asked for it.

GANTON

It is really necessary to have a car as there is no accommodation in the immediate neighbourhood. There are, of course, masses of hotels in Scarborough, which is about ten miles away, and there is a frequent bus service which passes through Ganton village, five minutes' walk from the club house.

The food at the club is absolutely first-rate.

There are always caddies to be had, and a *Caddy-master* who will look after you wonderfully well, and if humanly possible get you a game if you are alone.

Green fees, April to September: 5s. a day; 10s. Saturday; £1 Sunday or Bank Holidays; £2 10s. a week; £4 a month. October to April the differences are: 10s. Sunday; 30s. a week; £3 a month.

GLENEAGLES

Unless you are staying at the Gleneagles Hotel a car is essential.

There is plenty of accommodation in *Auchterarder*, which is a mile or so away: Ruthven Hall Hotel; Collearn Castle Hotel; Crown; Queen's; Star; Station.

The Gleneagles Hotel itself is open from Easter to October, and guests play at reduced green-fee rates.

For visitors: 6s. a day; 7s. 6d. Saturday; 10s. Sunday.

But for this you can play on the King's and Queen's and Prince's courses.

There are always caddies to be had, and an excellent lunch and tea at the club house.

HARLECH, *Royal St. David's*

Harlech stands on the hill, the links is below. This is important if you have no car, for it is a *very* steep hill and they do not serve lunch at the golf club, only tea. Therefore, unless you want to climb the hill for your lunch, take sandwiches with you.

But: The Queen's Hotel is in the flat, nearest to the links; The Castle is, oddly enough, next to the castle on the hill-top; The St. David's half-way up, but a little farther away.

However, if you have a car all is well.

The station is close to the club, and one can take a train along to Aberdovey, or vice versa, if you want a change.

APPENDIX

Green fees, April to end of October: 7s. 6d. a day; 37s. 6d. a week; £4 10s. a month. November to end of March: 5s. a day; 30s. a week; £3 a month.

Remember that there is *no Sunday opening* of pubs.

HOYLAKE, *Royal Liverpool*

To play at Hoylake it is necessary to be introduced by a member of the club. It is no use turning up as a chance visitor.

There is no need for a car once you are there.

The Royal (Golf) Hotel; The Stanley; The Green Lodge. All these are within very easy walking distance from the first tee.

Green fees: 7s. 6d. weekdays; £1 Saturday, Sunday, Bank Holidays, Good Friday, Christmas Day, and Competition days.

HUNSTANTON

The golf links is about a mile from the town.

The Lestrange Arms and Golf Hotel is only about three minutes away from the club house.

The next nearest is the Lodge Hotel in Old Hunstanton.

In the town is the Golden Lion.

The railway service via Cambridge and King's Lynn is not noted for speed.

One should bring an introduction from one's own club secretary or a member.

An excellent lunch and tea can be had at the club.

Green fees: 6s. a round; 10s. a day; £2 a week; £3 5s. a fortnight; £4 5s. three weeks; £5 a month. There are certain reductions for family parties.

At Easter, Whitsun, and August Bank Holidays the green fee is £1 a day, or 7s. 6d. after 4 p.m.

Whilst at Hunstanton you will hear talk of its neighbour *Brancaster*. It is well worth a visit! Then you will be able to argue, too. I'm not saying another word.

LITTLE ASTON

One of the difficulties of Little Aston is where to stay. You may stay, if you like, in Birmingham, or there is the Royal Hotel at Sutton Coldfield, which is the nearest, or there is Lichfield, about eight miles away, which is the most attractive place.

Anyway, you will need a car.

There is excellent food at the club. It is best to order lunch when you arrive for the morning round.

Caddies are available, and for these days, very reasonable.

APPENDIX

Green fees: 10s. a day; £1 Saturday and Sunday. (These fees are halved if you are playing with a member.)

Ladies are not allowed to play on Saturdays at all, and not till 2.30 on Sundays.

MOORTOWN

Moortown, and its neighbour Sand Moor, are both on the main Harrogate road on the very edge of Leeds. There are plenty of hotels in Harrogate, which is about eight miles off, and half-way there is the Harewood Arms in the village of Harewood.

Being on the main road there is an excellent bus service either way, at fifteen-minute intervals.

Good lunch and tea can be had at the club.

Green fees: 7s. 6d. a day; 10s. Wednesdays; £1 Saturday, Sunday, and public holidays.

Whilst in the vicinity, *Alwoodley* is a course to visit.

MUIRFIELD

To play on the links of the Honourable Company of Edinburgh Golfers one must be introduced by a member.

Muirfield is at Gullane, and for a golfing holiday the place is ideal.

There are Gullane Nos. 1, 2, and 3. There is New Luffness.

There is plenty of accommodation, including: Grey Walls Hotel (next to the Muirfield club house); Marine Hotel; Bissett's Hotel; Queen's Hotel; Golf Hotel.

Gullane is about eighteen miles from Edinburgh and there is a half-hourly bus service, quarter-hourly in summer, right to the first tee of Gullane No. 1, and to within three minutes of Muirfield.

Muirfield is 10s. a day; £1 at weekends.

Gullane No. 1: 7s. 6d. and 10s.; Gullane No. 2: 3s. 6d. a round; 6s. a day (Sundays included). Gullane No. 3: 2s. 6d. a round; 4s. a day (Sundays included).

Buses start from St. Andrew Square in Edinburgh.

It is not advisable to attempt to reach Gullane by train.

Food in Gullane is easily procurable. Food at Muirfield is of course excellent, once one is admitted.

NORTH BERWICK

There is such a range of hotel and boarding-house accommodation that it is probably best to write to the Town Clerk with particulars of your requirements.

This is an ideal family place. The beaches are splendid and the bathing safe. In the season you must always book your starting-time, but it is nearly always possible to start between 1.15 and 1.45, and this is recommended to any chance comer.

There is a good train service from Edinburgh as well as buses.

No Sunday play on the West course (Old course). Sunday play on the Burgh course.

Green fees, *West Course:* November to May: 3s. a day; 15s a week; 35s. a month. June: 4s. a day; 18s. a week; 40s. a month. July to September: 5s. a day; 20s. a week; 40s. a month. October: 4s. a day; 18s. a week; 40s. a month.

Food and drink must be obtained in the town.

PORTRUSH

Portrush is about an hour and twenty minutes by train from Belfast.

The links is half a mile out of the town, but for the weary there always seem to be taxis available.

Caddies are reasonable and efficient.

There are special green-fee terms for those staying at the Northern Counties Hotel.

Green fees: 5s. a day; 10s. at weekend; 30s. a week; 85s. a month.

Besides the Dunluce links there is also the Valley course, which is right under the lee of the dunes and sheltered from the wind.

RYE

You need an introduction from your golf-club secretary or from a member.

The course is three miles out of Rye on the road to Camber. There is a good bus service which starts from the station yard and runs about twenty-minutely in summer and less in winter. (Bus no. 114 East Kent, a red bus.)

The George Hotel; The Monastery Guest House. If you have a car there is Pelsham at Iden, three miles inland.

For *weekenders:* There is one good train down from London at 5 p.m. from Cannon Street, arr. Rye 6.38. There is also a reasonable train back on Sunday at 6.1 p.m., getting to Charing Cross at 8.15, or an early Monday-morning one at 7.46, arriving Cannon Street at 9.30.

Excellent lunch and tea except Tuesdays.

Green fees: 7s. 6d. a day; 10s Sundays (£1 if introduced by letter).

ST. ANDREWS

If you are intending to stay during the season it is necessary to book well in advance.

Rusack's Marine Hotel; Athol Hotel; Royal Hotel; Golf Hotel; Station and Windsor; Links Hotel; Cross Keys Hotel; Scores Hotel.

APPENDIX

These are not the only hotels. As usual, in Scotland food must be obtained in the town if one is a day visitor.

On the Old course starting is by ballot from June to September. (It is likely you will visit St. Andrews during this period.) There is *no* ballot for the three other courses.

Green fees, Old course: 3s. 6d. a round; New course: 2s. a round; Eden course: 2s. a round; Jubilee: 1s. a round; Play on Sundays on the Eden only: 4s. a round.

St. Andrews is reachable fairly circuitously by train, but it is almost worth coming that way so as to arrive looking out at the Eden, and then at the Old course. The Old course is on your left and the holes you will see closest are the 15th and 16th. But you will see the whole stretch of country on which the Old, New, and Jubilee are laid out.

SUNNINGDALE

The village is on the main London–Portsmouth road. If you are coming from London by car, turn first left just over the level-crossing up a hill and the drive in to the club is only about three hundred yards along, on the left.

The same applies if you arrive by train. The service from Waterloo is frequent and the journey takes between forty-five and fifty-five minutes. It'll take about that by car, too.

The Sunningdale Hotel is just the London side of the level-crossing, and therefore very convenient.

Green fees: 10s. a round; £1 at weekend.

You need an introduction from a member or from your club secretary.

WALTON HEATH

The station for Walton Heath is Tadworth, which can be reached from Charing Cross or London Bridge in about three-quarters of an hour. From Tadworth station it is about a mile and a bit to the club house, but it is usually possible to get a taxi on the spot, or with very little waiting.

By car it is not too easy to find, but the road to aim for when in the vicinity is B.2032. You can make the outer approach from Epsom, Sutton, or Purley, or by way of Kingston and Leatherhead. A map is a good thing.

The Heath Guest House is the nearest hotel; there is also the Lodge Hotel at Chipstead.

An introduction from a member or your club secretary is necessary.

Green fees: 10s. a day; £1 at weekend. If playing with a member these fees are halved.

Excellent food.

APPENDIX

WESTWARD HO! *Royal North Devon*

You cannot get farther than Bideford by train. But from there, there are frequent buses and the journey takes only twenty minutes. Once at Westward Ho! you're bound to be reasonably near the links, so that a car is not essential.

Excellent lunch and tea at the club. Caddies available.

Green fees; 5s. a day; 25s. a week; 70s. a month.

Dormy House Hotel; Golden Bay Hotel.

WORLINGTON AND NEWMARKET

You *can* get to Worlington Halt by train from Cambridge. It takes about three-quarters of an hour and the service is not frequent! Really a car is essential.

Coming through Newmarket keep straight on, on the Thetford road (A.11), for about five miles and then turn sharp left at a cross-roads which is signposted. About a couple of miles down this you will see ahead a humpbacked railway bridge. Just before you reach it, turn sharp right, and there you are. If you are coming any other way I expect you know the way.

Green fees: 5s. a day; 10s. at weekend. You get reduced fees if playing with a member, and you need in the first instance to be introduced by one.

Bull Hotel, Barton Mills; Bell Hotel, Mildenhall; Turk's Head, Beck Row. There are also hotels in Newmarket.

Excellent lunch and tea at club.